Gleanings of an Old Geechee

Gleanings of an Old Geechee

Bill Bowen

Library of Congress Control Number: 2012914999
ISBN: Hardcover   978-1-4797-0212-1
                    Softcover   978-1-4797-0211-4
                    Ebook   978-1-4797-0213-8

To order additional copies of this book, contact:
Xlibris Corporation
1-888-795-4274
www.Xlibris.com
Orders@Xlibris.com
119145

Contents

Geechee: **One born and raised in Low Country**, South Carolina, and who speaks the dialect.

Foreword

These anecdotes, poems, and short stories were written for my own enjoyment, and now, as I grow older, I want to share them with you. As I attain this stage of my life, that of being a curmudgeon, perhaps my desire for some form of immortality is the force that encourages me to put this book together.

Further, as I hear my friends gather for coffee and tell wonderful stories of their past lives, I realize that there are many more books waiting to be written. I encourage you to find some way to record your own thoughts and memories. Perhaps a journal will be your method. If we do not record those extraordinary stories, when we grandparents leave this world, our future families will never hear them.

Billy Bigelow (in the musical carousel) after his death said to St. Peter, "Well, I guess that's the end of my life on earth"!

The gatekeeper replied, "As long as one person loves you, it shall not end!"

Bill

Acknowledgments

Thank you:

to my wife June (Island Girl) for her encouragement, inspiration, and for taking initiative to put this product of my imagination into a readable source

to my granddaughter Brittany for helping this computer-ignorant "Goggy"

to my senior friends who encourage my writings in *Letters to the Editor*

to the Shepherds Center's creative writing programs, especially the ones at Trenholm Road, which allowed me to teach my love for books

to Dottie and her prime-time writing program which encouraged my love for writing

to Lea, my fellow writing friend

to *The State* newspaper which have generously published many of my stories and letters

to Daphne and Clint at Xlibris

to my writing hero, Lewis Grizzard.

Lowcountry

Honor! Pride! Arrogance?

Why are the *Low Country* (Charleston) folks different from the rest of the state and country?

Charleston was originally settled and governed by the aristocrats of Europe. Because of *indigo, rice, and cotton,* many of those who were neither aristocratic nor rich rapidly became so and adopted their social and political lifestyle. Thus, they made their own rules. Though we were occupied by the "Red Coats" and the Yankees, they could take our land but, as in *Fiddler on the Roof,* never our *traditions!*

We continued to "Unto our own selves be true." We made our own rules (while others made laws, which we collectively ignored if we wished). What did they mean . . . "pash" . . . they were "country bumpkins" sent here by the German-British alliance to protect United States from the Indians and potential slave uprisings. Other than a few aristocrats like John C. Calhoun, most of the others were Tories (traitors) who fought for the British during the Revolution. Did you know that in the decisive battles of *Cowpens, Ninety Six, and Kings Mountain* the only *British* fighting for the crown were a couple of *Red coat officers?* The rest were Tories. (Americans fighting for the English cause.) They try to justify their position by stating, the fact, that this land was *given* to them by the Crown, who had earned their loyalty. They were relatively small landowners who were not concerned with *stamp taxes,* etc., so this was not their problem!

You see, this was the only true *Civil War.* The one in 1860 was fought between two sovereign nations: the USA and the CSA (Confederate States of America), while the Revolutionary War was fought between our own citizens over whether to continue to accept the laws created by *England* or not.

So why are *we* so independent? Because *we* won that war, more battles of the Revolution were fought in South Carolina than all of the other states combined. *We* are *gentlemen and ladies* and believe in the Sin Lancelot brand of *chivalry* as a lifestyle; we overcame the harshest occupation ever conducted by a defeated enemy of the USA, battered but never broken, and *honor and pride* are still most important to us. No one will ever take our independence because we remain united as an ***independent society*** in spite of the scalawags like that 10 percent of the Citadel Cadet Corps who can't handle the little touch of authority they experience in *hazing* underclassmen and a few writers like Pat Conroy, the misguided talent.

So we live by our own liquor laws, blue laws, prostitution laws, and social laws. We dance to the tune of a different drummer because that is our "God-given right!"

Low Country Ambience

It was a typical spring morning on the corner of Broad and Meeting Streets in downtown Charleston, South Carolina. The only folks stirring were a few lawyers and interns who were trying to make it to Starbucks and their caffeine high. Well, there were a few others who were just coming home from a night on the town.

The slight offshore breeze combined the odors from the ocean with the fragrance of the wisteria and magnolia to create a perfume that, if she could duplicate it, Coco Chanel could market as Charleston Spring and make even more millions.

The morning sun shone through the oaks, palmettos, blooming azaleas, and camellias, while the shadows of the wind-driven Spanish moss created the likenesses of the haints, spirits, and ghosts, which gave Charleston the reputation of being a mysterious, if not haunted city.

Adding to the spirit of the morning is the quiet humming of the flower and basket ladies who were setting up their wares along the brick wall that protected the privacy of Saint Michaels Church Cemetery. Once in a while, someone would quietly begin the verse of the old spiritual: "I gotta a robe. You gotta a robe All God's chillin got a robe." Then quietly the group joins in: "When I git to heaven gonna put on ma robe and walk all over God's heaven." To add to the spirit of the occasion, often the chimes in the highest steeple in the city would peal out the notes of a familiar hymn.

More than three-quarters of a century ago, God chose to allow me the distinct honor to be born in the "holy city" of Charleston, South Carolina. Though we were not aristocrats, just being born there and speaking the language or "pat-wah" made us—in our own eyes at least—a little above the rest of the world. We lived as we pleased as we chose to ignore any laws, like the liquor laws and the blue laws, which created for us any inconvenience.

Though there was a class distinction in Charleston society, it did allow coexistence and mutual respect as Charlestonians among the blue-collar workers with their oyster roasts; the upper class, their Saint Andrews

Society; and the blacks, their rip-roaring church-related activities. Of course, occasionally some interloper, snob, drunk, or "redneck" would break the peace, but they were quickly dealt with by a group of their peers.

An outsider would be treated with courtesy and some respect, if they earned it. But they would never be considered an equal even to the lowest native-born Charlestonian. Though they might be occasional guests, try as they might, membership in the local blue-collar or black folks clubs was unusual. Membership in the Yacht Club, the Hibernians and Saint Andrews Society of the upper crust was never attainable

It was and is a city that radiates a certain European charm through its traditions, architecture, narrow streets, and alleys, especially in that area which begins at our financial district better known as "below Broad" and ends with the old mansions which overlook the battery. That area is better known as the "historic district" by the guides who drive the sightseers through that area in their horse-drawn carriages.

Adding to that charm was Rosa, a very special flower lady. All who saw her were taken by her dignified beauty as it added to the ambience of the corner by the wall that surrounded old Saint Michael's cemetery. As an aside, Boston's Old North Church had nothing on us as we too had our "one if by land two if by sea" in Saint Michael's steeple. Though some arrogant Bostonians claim that our Paul Revere was a sharecropper on a mule, what do they know?

Being surrounded by her bunches of flowers and sweet grass baskets made her appear as a real-life image of one of Mrs. Elizabeth O'Neill Verner's world-class watercolor paintings. Her black skin shone as would the paint on a newly polished limousine. Her teeth were as white as newly fallen snow. Her ample bosom seemed to be inviting a grandmother-like hug from anyone who was brave enough to risk the danger of being smothered in her cleavage.

Breaking the tranquility of the morning, the singsong sounds of the hucksters hawking their goods could be heard as they rolled their rickety wobbly-wheeled carts through the streets—"Frimpy frimpy da fresh! I catch 'em dis monin. Git yo supper heah. I got da flounder, da porgy, da spot, da croker and da Shak stake. Ya kno, shak stake don need no graby . . . put 'em in da pot, make his own grabby.

"Mornin', Mr. Mayor, please take dis daisy to the misses in the hospital."

"Oh, thank you, Rosa, and I better take that wildflower assortment too"

"Thank ya, sih, and tell her to git well soon and have a big party so Rosa can furnish dem flowers. God bless ya, Mr. Mayor!"

"Good mornin' Pastor! Ya know, I pass right by huh las Sunday on the way to my church, and I hear ya preachin' up a storm. And I say to myself *Amen* when I hear you tell 'em dat day goin' straight to hell if they don't put on dat cloak of rightness and walk a chalk line! Yes, sih, Amen!" Now, Pastor, don't forget tomorrow yo anniversary, and you betta git da misses something or you be sleepin' on da daybed. I got this pretty little basket for her to put on the dressa to hold her jewelry at night while y'all sleep."

"Well, Rosa, you just saved my life. I don't need for the misses to be mad with me. I don't cook so well ya know."

"Thank ya, and please give the misses my love."

"Yes, 'em, I make all this basket myself. My boy, go out and gather da sweet grass and palms and bring 'em home to me, and I make da basket. No two jus alike. You don't talk like U from Charleston!"

"Yes, we're down for a visit from New York City."

"Oh, dat is sho a long way from Charleston. Do they make sweet grass basket there?" "No, I'm afraid not. We import most of our things from across the ocean."

"Look, I'm in kind of a hurry, so I might come back later and look some more. But in the meantime, I think I'll take that large basket with the handle. It'll look beautiful full of roses or glads in my foyer."

"Yes, mam it sho will. Tank ya, misses. When ya look at dat basket in yo home, think of good times you have in dis "holy city" and please, ma'am, don't forget Rosa sittin' right here by dis churchyard. Tank ya, ma'am, and God bless ya, ma'am!"

"Hey, Mr. Senator, guess you bin busy in Washington. We miss ya when you not sittin' in your seat. Day say President George Washington sat there when he was in dis town a long time ago."

"Well, Rosa, I've had to go out of the country a whole lot since we got involved with this war. And speaking of that, you see that lady coming to the church with that little girl and boy?"

"Yas, sa, I see 'em!"

"Well, when she comes by, give her that bunch of flowers and just tell her thank-you! You see, about a week ago, her husband, the father of those children, was killed in the war. And, oh yes, Rosa, if she asks where they came from, just tell her that they are from all of us who appreciate the gift she gave to save our freedom."

"Yas, sir, I sho will, and I'll give each of the little chillin' a basket if dat's OK."

"Yes, and thank you, Rosa."

"Tank ya, sir. I pray that you'll be safe flyin' all ova in dat airplane . . . And God bless ya, Mr. Senator."

"Pastor, what can we do? The folks are so slow coming in for the Palm Sunday services we're gonna run late."

"Well, Deacon, be patient, Rosa's at it again. She's giving everyone a piece of a palm branch to lay down in the isle for the processional."

Headline in the *Charleston News and Courier—Out of Control Tour Bus Crashes into Front of Old Church.*

With the muted grandiose organ setting the mood of the occasion while quietly playing selected pieces from Handel's Messiah, the black limousines unloaded the important officials who joined the everyday citizens awaiting the beginning of the memorial service. Everyone in attendance had been given a wild flower by the ladies who sat at the church cemetery wall. Each attendee stood and held their flower respectfully as the floral spray-draped casket and the family passed down the long aisle to their respective places at the front of the church.

The music, eulogies, and sermon formulated a service fit for the loved and well-respected one for whom it was intended.

The service ended with the all-black choir rendering the old spiritual: "I know the Lord. I know the Lord laid His hands on me . . . He healed the sick and raised the dead. I know the Lord laid His hands on me."

Strains of the glorious Hallelujah Chorus resonated through the place as the family and the congregation followed the casket. Leading the way was the large sweet grass and wild flower wreath dissected by a ribbon bearing the words *rest in peace . . . Rosa . . . rest in peace!*

Keep Talkin'

During the slow tourist season in the Low Country, the Charleston Tourist Bureau or some such organization offers a program to encourage hometown folks to see the historical sites and gardens. And to accomplish that they offer a pass for a one-time fee of $10. Being a couple of Charlestonians and not having enjoyed the beauty of those places in a long time, June, my wife, and I got her sister and a cousin to get a family pass which more than fulfilled its purpose by affording us a delightful two-day journey into the past. Being kinfolks, I'm sure that we shared a communing of spirits with our forefathers, while recognizing that we were enjoying their times through the preservation of the properties of their contemporary but much more opulent coexisters.

Some of the more notable stops on our jaunt were the majestic Boone Hall "a living" Plantation, the elegant presumptuously wealth-flaunting architecture of the Nathaniel Russell House, perusing—that means strolling in Charlestonese—the ghost-filled alleys near the Battery, the ancient landscaped gardens of Middleton Place, and the informal beauty of "magnificent" Magnolia Gardens.

It was truly a beautiful trek through the past. But as pretty as were the landscapes, it was a person whom I met while at Magnolia that creates the fondest memories of the excursion.

While waiting for my fellow adventurers to finish their shopping spree, I made myself comfortable on the "jostlin' board" outside the gift shop. I must have been in deep thought contemplating the events that might have transpired right on this spot in the past few hundred years because I jumped when I was startled by a voice. "How ya doin' there, Bossman?" As I looked up, I saw that the speaker was a little old man sitting on a bench with a paintbrush in his hand. He appeared to be one of those ageless personalities whom "the powers that be" can't bear to let go and keep around just because "it's the thing to do." My answer of "just fine thanks and how are you, sir?" began a conversation that lasted more than thirty minutes that passed until the girls reappeared.

Though the conversation was interesting, I could not help but notice that not once during all that time did his brush touch the long wrought iron fence, which he was apparently supposed to be painting. But whatever either of us should have been doing and did not accomplish it was still a mutually pleasant repose.

As we parted and said our good-byes, he asked me for the time. I replied, "It's just about 2:45 p.m." With that, our final communication was his response, "Thank goodness . . . 'cause at 3:30 p.m., I get my 'break!'"

Gleanings from Edisto

Sunrise and Sunset,
Beginning and the end.
Alpha and omega.
While life and death emend.

Beach and mud flat.
Hatchings of all life.
Creeks and river branches.
Highways to ocean strife.

Mullet and brown shrimp.
Tastes which some folks tout.
Humans with a net.
Compete with porpoises and trout.

Cockles and sand dollars,
Decorate the shore.
Beauty from a home.
Where life exists no more.

Raccoon and beachcomber.
Walk the strand with muse.
Different from each other.
One for food, the other to peruse.

Estuary and cemetery.
A microcosm of space.
Of beauty or of bleak.
A choice we must embrace.

Ashepoo, Combahee, and Edisto

(Feeding the Ace Basin)

A virgin forest of oaks, gums, and
Long leaf pines standing over coffee colored,
Tannin stained creeks flowing
Thru the sand of a long receded sea,
Uncaringly navigating to the bright blue
Yawning expanse of the Atlantic!

My Love
Lovely evening sky.
Beauty of God's blessed love.
My June Byrd Bowen.

Polishing the Old Apple
My fellow writers.
Students of lore I adore.
Gather to compose.

Freedom
All it takes is for good men to do naught
For evil to grow and be allowed
While freedom flies out the door
And in vain all the battles were fought.

Adoration
Praise God!
With songs and prayers,
His blessings shine upon us,
With love and grace beyond compare.
He cares!

Peace of Mind

The young people think that eighty years
Is a mighty long time.
And for many folks it is.

Especially those whose life is one of torment
As they search for the impossible dream
Of all the riches they desire.

But then we can not leave out their
Quest for all thing of pleasure
And the o-pe-nt of that obsession.

In that many years if I attained any bits of wisdom
This old folk will gladly share
And pass it on to you . . .

Follow God's law and you will reap
The rewards of not only the hereafter
'Cause He will give you so much more.

Heaven can begin right here on earth.
In spite of all the worlds ordeals
Of awesome trials and tribulations.

If nobody knows da troubles you've seen but Jesus
He offers heaven and earthly peace of mind
And, my friend, that's quite enough.

Musings While Joggling on a Jostlin' Board

Writer's block has a hold on me and will not let go. I have sat for hours at my desk (a hundred-year-old oak library table that was a wedding gift to my wife's grandma). What to do? Class is coming up, and I have nothing, not even a thought . . . Gasp . . . , the impending embarrassment is not something to which I look forward.

The sound of thunder and the much-needed water falling from the sky woke me from my nonproductive despair. I could not resist going out on the front porch to sit and watch the rain while gently bouncing on the "jostlin' board."

Maybe I need to tell you non-geechees just what is a jostlin' board. It's a piece of furniture which I've never seen any place except on porches and piazzas in Charleston, South Carolina. The board is a twelve-inch-wide sixteen-foot-long yellow pine plank that hangs loosely with two pegs on each end holding it to the top of two four-foot tall rockers. We called them jostlin' boards long before they inflated the price by several hundred dollars and named them joggling boards. Whatever be the name, they do the same thing—you know, that "rose by any other name" bit.

Though children play on them, perhaps they are better used during the courtship ritual. At the beginning of the date, the lovers sit the "respectable" distance apart. The up and down movement of the board with its bending in the middle moves the bodies closer and closer until they . . . err umm until they . . . "Oh, my weak heart" . . . until they actually touch.

The rhythm of my movement on the board, the symphony created by the rain's melodious fall through the leaves, the harmony of it bouncing off the metal gutters, and the bass accents of the thunder put me in a nostalgic trance that brought back many wonderful memories of a boyhood that could not have been better.

As devout Jews yearn for Jerusalem, Muslims for Mecca, and Hindus for the Ganges; we Charlestonians cling to our Low Country heritage. Though June and I made the supreme sacrifice by migrating to the Piedmont and eventually to the Midlands in order to build a business, our hearts still remain in "the Holy City."

I believe where our heart is, there too are our most precious thoughts and memories. Mine are of wonderful anecdotes in an area of this universe that is as close to heaven as can be found. The building of a life, as in a structure, must have a strong foundation. I was blessed!

If I had occasion to pout, Mama would usually say, "Now, Billy, who licked the red off your candy."

Daddy said that he never bet again after, as a young man, he lost 50 cents to a fellow who bet he could take Daddy's vest off without first taking off Daddy's coat.

Granddaddy would say that he was "all stove up" because of the overuse of his ancient muscles.

"I swear" was not acceptable language in our home, but "I swanee" was just fine, especially for the ladies. Grandma Bowen might say, "I declare."

Grandma Shingler always called "red bud" trees "Judas trees" because they usually bloomed first in the spring. That privilege was supposed to be reserved for the dogwood from which Christ's cross was made.

Look at that little ragamuffin was the usual comment when viewing an unkempt street urchin.

Yes, it was a simple time, a time of grocery shopping for the basics at Mr. Hockimeyer's Corner Grocery. He was a wiz at wrapping the meat in paper taken from a large roll and tying it with string that was pulled through bent nails in the ceiling. Though he had a little trouble separating his English speaking from his native German, he had no trouble figuring the whole grocery bill on a piece of butcher paper with the stub of a pencil.

The local fresh seafood was purchased from the vendors who pushed their carts through the streets. The two-wheelers were rickety with wiggly metal wheels that caused their hanging scales to sway back and forth in the rhythm of the seas from which came their cargo. Those who did not have scales, they sold their wares by the plate.

Vegetables and fruits were hung or placed all over the carts or horse-drawn wagons and were sold by the bunch or basket. So often a vendor would add an extra fish or tomato "for brodus." "For brodus" was for free and a reminder to do business with the giver the next time they passed through. And we knew when they were coming as we could hear them shouting their wares from blocks away . . . frimpee (shrimp) . . . blu crab . . . wedgitable (note: the w replaces the v) . . . got yo red mato rite hare . . . shak (shark) stak don need no graby (gravy) put e in da pot make e on graby Oista oista (oyster) . . . stew em . . . roastem . . . da mak ya strong . . . give ya nice baby . . . frimpee . . . blu crab . . . oista . . . oista . . . weg-a-tible!

The arrival of the iceman, in his horse-drawn wagon, was much anticipated as he always seemed to arrive just as the family was running out of coolant. The sign displayed in the front window of his customer's home told him how much ice was needed. With his pick moving faster than a hungry woodpecker's bill, he would chip away the right amount from the giant block in his sawdust-strewn wagon, put it on his massive leather-covered shoulder, carry it up the stairs, and deposit in the icebox. He and the milkman's movements were monitored closely. Their actions created lots of conversation among the ladies about in whose kitchen they stayed the longest. The kids love him because he shared the slivers left over from the chipping.

It was a time of innocence, of love thy neighbor, a time of giving and getting from friends and family, yes, a time of water and a meal to the hobo (of either race) who swept the front sidewalk. Sometimes it was cleaned several times in the same day. We, who had little, gave willingly to those who had less.

Amy Lowell, in selected lines (with my slight paraphrase) from her poem entitled Charleston South Carolina, wrote about "my city." Perhaps it also says something about me.

> O loveliness of old, decaying, haunted things!
> little streets untouched, shamefully paved,
> Full of mist and fragrance on this rainy evening.
> "You should have come at dawn, said my friend,
> "and seen the orioles, and thrushes, and mockingbirds in the garden."
>
> "Yes," I said absentmindedly,
> As I felt the sharp touch of ivy upon my hand which rested against the wall.
> But I thought to myself,
> "There is no dawn here, only sunset,
> And an evening rain scented with flowers"!

Neighbors and Friends

Memo

To: Timberlake Golf Club Board of Directors
From: George Kerison

Subject: "Tinkling"

Text: As you most likely know, our home is in the pine grove about one hundred yards above the twelfth green. My wife Joannie finds it offensive that the men golfers "tinkle" behind the trees all along the fairways leading to the twelfth and thirteenth holes.

We insist that you advise us ASAP what you plan to do to solve this problem for Joannie. Do not force us to take further action to resolve this situation to our satisfaction!

Memo

To: Mr. George Kerison
From: Timberlake Golf Club Board of Directors

Subject: Offending Mrs. Joannie Kerison

Text: Being a golfer yourself, you must understand, with the scarcity of bathrooms on the course, that keeping the male golfers from "watering the trees" creates an almost insurmountable problem. So if we are going to be able to satisfy your demand to keep Joannie from being offended, we will need your complete cooperation by asking you to . . . take away Joannie's binoculars!

Bill Bowen

Why is it at Timberlake they are known as palmetto bugs, while in the "holy city" of Charleston, in the ghettos housing the minorities and the mansions housing the "below broad aristocrats" alike, they're simply known as roaches?

Ramblings

While playing golf with my friend, *Ham*, he was in a *sand trap* in each of the first five and seven of the last nine holes. Every time, he was able to get out of the trap very well using only one stroke.

Does that make him a *prolific or a proficient sand player* or both? Will a good English scholar please step forward?

Remember when *divorce* was not so prevalent and a divorced lady was sometimes referred to as a *grass widow!*

While looking for a parking place at the bank, the only vacant space was marked *handicapped* only. I rode around the block several times and finally discovered a *handicapped person* parked in a regular parking space.

Should I be *ashamed* for being a little angry?

While discussing our *cruise* to the West Indies, the *preacher's wife* listened attentively but remarked that "he would never go."

Trying to be "helpful," I sent her a copy of the beautiful *Royal Caribbean cruise line* brochure. The Sunday following the reception of that packet, he said to me, "You certainly are getting me in *deep water*." Chuckle, chuckle. To this, I replied, "I can't *FATHOM* anyone not wanting to cruise!" (*ta da*—there's those drums again)

The best wedding present I can think of would be one that was accompanied by a prewritten *thank-you note* and a *self-addressed stamped envelope* so that all the bride has to do is sign it, put it in the envelope, and mail it. Try it—she will love it!

At my age, I can never be sure what kind of an evening I had. However, if I wake up and my *night shirt* is on wrong-side-out, I'm almost sure "*I had a ball.*"

Old Age is Not Necessarily the Pits!

A lot of so-called experts including Art Linkletter have written books about getting old. His was called *Old Age is Not for Sissies*. I believe that, but I'm here to tell you that no matter what he and his money-making published author and expert cronies try to tell you about aging, if it includes getting out of this thing alive, it is a bald-faced lie. A few thousand years ago, a couple of folks almost made it but, to paraphrase Mr. Gray in his famous eulogy, the paths of glory still led "but to the grave." George Gershwin also covered the subject very well in his operetta Porgy and Bess when he had Sportin' Life sing, "Methuselah lived nine hundred years but who calls dat livin' if no gals gonna give in to no man what's nine hundred years." And by the way, I read somewhere that Methuslah had a nagging wife and that's where the Lord got his ideas about *hell*. But that, of course, is another story.

Perhaps you'll forgive me if you've heard this story that's been going around for sometime, but it is relevant to the point I'm trying to make.

Though several years ago, my friend Dave thought that he had permanently handled his hearing problem by mechanical means, he was surprised when he suddenly became as deaf as a post again. After much aggravation by his wife, he finally went to the doctor where the physician concluded that Dave had a suppository stuck in his ear. Dave's reaction was a relieved, "Who . . . oo boy, that is good news. Now I know where I put my hearing aid."

I really don't have a major problem with this getting old bit as long as I remember to take my arthritis strength aspirin, my Metamusel for regularity, cranberry juice to add a few more minutes between trips to the bathroom, a Ginseng pill for . . . hum a . . . for . . . well, umm . . . well, let's put it like this, Ginseng is an oriental herb taken by men in Asia and there certainly are a lot of little Chinese children running around, and lastly the Beano and/ or Gas-X must not be forgotten if we are to have a quiet evening at home. I am apparently not the only one who appreciates that scientific miracle, for according to a recent TV commercial, Beano is the drug of choice with the Trapest, who lives under a vow of silence, in their monastery at Moncks Corner, South Carolina.

I don't believe in messing with the hard stuff, but I do believe that the legitimate over the counter elixirs found at the local drug store are the "God's send" that can make this aging process, if not fun, then at least tolerable.

A lot of togetherness, the "College of Hard Knocks," and some time generated wisdom has given most of us the background which allows for the understanding and tolerance toward our spouses that cuts down on so many of the tensions that exists among our younger married friends. A good example of that kind of older relationship is the following somewhat true anecdote. Paul, a quiet retired mechanical engineer, and Doris, a typical outgoing, southern, shopaholic wife and mother are a good example of that. Though in their seventies, Doris has continued, yes, not only continued but has recently become even more enthusiastic in her daily jogging regimen. It includes the ritual of putting on her running shoes and exercise outfit every morning and going for about an hour's spin around the neighborhood. All went very well with that until a few days ago when Paul made an enlightening discovery while searching for her due to a minor emergency at home. Instead of finding her padding along the asphalt as a runner, rather he saw her sheepishly exiting a neighbor's house. Being stubborn and feeling pretty secure in their almost fifty-year marriage, Doris decided that explanations were unnecessary, and Paul, though extremely curious, did not want to appear to be the jealous husband, just kept his mouth shut. Nothing changed the stubborn and curious status quo until that evening, when during one of the more violent thunderstorms of the season, a very large pine tree fell on their house. Since this was the second tree to hit them in less than a year, Doris really became afraid, no, not just afraid, Doris, as we say in the South, got "flat scared." She thought that the other occasion was a warning, but this time, the tree was so large and the tempest so fierce, she felt that God was out to get her for her deceptions and that she had better get her life in order and quickly. So, in an attempt to relieve some of the pangs of guilt, she started to confess the confession of a deceiver.

It seems that there was a well-organized secret catalog club on her jogging route. She and the rest of the club members would take turns stopping in houses to shop. They had good set up with one home featuring Neiman Marcus, another Macy's, another Sak's, and so on. The only hitch in the organization was that Doris's contribution to the club was to have been the Victoria's Secret catalog, but she could never find her copies. As an aside, a few days after the incident, while helping Paul clean up his basement workshop, she found the lost copies on a secluded back shelf. But that too is another story.

Though Doris's disclosures of the clandestine shopping operation created some serious problems in the home life of some of the younger families, all turned out very well for them as Paul had learned long ago that if he "kept his head," just smiled and kept his mouth shut, he would be rewarded greatly with much peace and quiet.

Yes, the ability to laugh at oneself is very helpful in aging gracefully. I got my own best, though slightly puckered, chuckle just the other morning while in the bathroom without my glasses. While there, I quickly learned that it is better to be safe than sorry as I reversed the application area of my Fixodent dental adhesive and the Preparation H. Hemorrhoid Cream.

PS. Someone said that Preparation H. was also good for the bags under your eyes. But, I ask you, in order to get the stuff that high, wouldn't you have to squeeze the tube very hard?

To My Friend Whose Wife Suffers from Headaches!

Mr. George Simon

Dear George,

Thought you might be interested in the attached article that appeared in yesterday's paper.

Headache Cure?

Twenty-four percent of women in a recent study said they got relief from their migraines from having sex. Longevity magazine reports.

I hope you understand the ramifications of this, one of the great medical discoveries.

1. *You have ceased to become the cause of the headaches but are now the* cure.
2. *"I have a headache" no longer means "not tonight dear" but is now an invitation to an evening of romantic ecstasy.*
3. *You can have more time for golf. It will no longer be necessary for you to waste good daylight time with aerobic and weight lifting programs. You can now get all of the exercise you need in the evening.*
4. *Do you realize that instead of her having to take pills, that you are now the prescription.*

If this information is indeed correct, I know that you will have a truly happy New Year*!*

Best Wishes (you lucky devil)

Technical Letter
Migraine Headaches and Their Control
Quasi-Doctor W. Manley Bowen

It has come to my attention that as a result of my original technical letter concerning *migraines,* the overuse of the prescribed therapy has created what appears to be a cure. This is especially true when the female of the species is the one who has the headaches. The desired effect of the therapy is *control,* not cure. I take full responsibility for this overmedication since it occurred due to my miscalculation. As to the zeal of the mediator and the effectiveness of the medication, it stops all mention by the patient of any symptoms.

In order to alleviate the condition of extreme anxiety in one or more of the partners created by this *cure,* we offer this follow-up letter with the hope that it will solve any problems created by the aforementioned misreckoning.

To re-create migraine symptoms, I suggest the following:

1. As a part of your continuing education program, have the partner read—*presiding and maintaining decorum at the annual conference using the edition of Robert's Rules of Order as revised by the bishop.*
2. Ten minutes of listening to a high volume stereo rendition of Rap for Honkies by H. C. Hammer.
3. Have her spend an evening listening to a native of Newark telling how they do everything better in New Jersey.
4. Tell her that you invited your thirteen-year-old nephew to spend the summer with you all at the lake.
5. Cancel her credit cards without telling her.
6. Tell her you're having your ears pierced.

If all the above fail, take the enclosed mallet and tap her sharply right between the eyes.

If you are the man you think you are, she will offer her eternal gratitude, and the headaches will return on a regular basis without further external effort.

PS. You might as well cancel your cable as you won't be watching a lot of TV anymore.

Peggy

Peggy and June, my wife, have been friends since their early school years. They are like sisters who were popular, excellent students and good athletes all through high school.

Peggy married Marv, a young naval officer, who took her from Mt. Pleasant, South Carolina, to California via North Dakota. Thankfully, the friendship (which includes Marv and me) is so strong that it has endured the 3,000 miles and more than forty years of separation. We see each other about once per year as we try to get together on vacation and/or when Peggy comes back home, with or without Marv, to see her relatives.

Last summer when Peggy came for a visit, we picked her mama up from the Methodist Home, toured the old family places, and explored the family cemetery plots. The conversations were the traditional southern reminiscences that included character analysis and the heritage of most of the folks their relatives married. "Oh, her, I don't know why Cousin Harry got mixed up with that "white trash." Just where did that child get those dark eyes? That huzzy chased him shamelessly."

Though she had heard this type of front porch Southern country gossip all of her informative years, Peggy, showing her newfound West Coast enlightenment, became very self-righteousness. "How can you talk like that? What difference does it make who Aunt Sis married?"

So this was the inspiration for the writing of the following verse! In addition to whatever profound content you might find, you will also see why my poetry writing has been kept to a minimum. Well, here goes with apologies to H. W. Longfellow and his *song of Hiawatha*.

By the shores of Shem Creek waters,
Near the foaming ocean's beaches,
Lived a maid whose name is Peggy,
In historic Charleston County,
With her parents, Myrt and Percy.
Percy had a deep dark secret,
Which he carried to his grave,
That Peggy obviously did not know,
When she criticized our Southern ways,
Concerning "poor white trash,"
And those whose blood is mixed,
So Myrtle became a little miffed,
At her daughter's attitude,
And let the cat out of the bag.
Your daddy had some Indian blood,
A running through his veins,
Which brought the astonished statement,
"You never told me that!
But it just proves my every point,
How can you say we're better,
Since we're in the same position,
As those whom you criticize?"
Mama's quick reply,
Belied her eighty years,
Even though her sight is fading,
And her step has slowed a mite,
Her mind's as nimble as can be,
As she proved with this retort,
I must remind you, Peggy Jean,
When you question my conviction,
"'Tis you whose blood is racially mixed,
But certainly not mine."

Creative Writing

Ms. Eleanor Bedenbaugh, who taught school for more than fifty years, graciously agreed to teach a *creative writing* course in The Shepherd's Center program which meets at the Lowman Home in White Rock, South Carolina. Though a gentle somewhat quiet lady, she still exhibits the aura of authority that is synonymous with the schoolmarms of her era. Thus, any look of disappointment from the diminutive Ms. B did quickly bring my six-foot-210-lb frame down to its emotional knees.

One assignment she gave us was, before the next session to write a short story containing the five senses. I got preoccupied with fishing, golf, or some other thing that we sixty-two-year-old kids might do and just did not take the time to do the homework.

"Maybe she will forget about it and take another route this week!" But alas her first statement was "We're going to read our five senses stories this morning ... Any Volunteers?"

Thank goodness, Hermine read hers entitled *The Fog* and Bob and Halen recited their poems entitled *The Little Redheaded Clowns and One Splendid Moment* respectively .... allowing me to buy some time.

While these and a few more recitations were going on, I finished my story containing the five senses just in time to hear, "We have just enough time for one more story. Bill Bowen, will you read yours!" * * * (Yes! not?—it was not a question) So I read it, and it went like this:

What's that I *hear?* Oh, I *see*, it's a skunk. It *feels* so soft and silky, but it *smells* so bad I can almost *taste* it.

"Thank you, Mr. Bowen."

"*Wsshuee!*" I say with a sigh of relief.

Prostitution in the Casino

Though you stand blankly staring tawdry harlots all,
You still beckon with your glitter to all who might partake.
With your siren calls you offer merriment galore,
For just a smidgen, caring not for those whose life you break.

Your left hand reaches and seductively invites,
"Pull me closer, adore me, and taste of all my wares,
Turn me on. Light my lights. Spin me round and round.
Make me sing. Ring my bell, while forgetting all your cares."

Pick your favorite from the rows of gaudy and ornate,
They will dance for just a pittance . . . a nickel, quarter, or a buck,
While offering all their fruits which appear so damningly sweet,
But are as bitter as were Eve's which ran all mankind amuck.

Breasts of cherries, grapes and plums appear before your eyes,
In mind-boggling sequences which offer more than just a mite,
With promises to all who will ultimately lose,
While hoping that the slots will not prevail again tonight.

But they will!
They always do!

Edisto in Winter

February at the beach,
Doesn't make a lot of sense,
It's much too cold to swim,
So why go to the expense?

I guess you think I'm crazy,
Because it is my favorite time,
To walk the strand and be alone,
Is being dif-fer-ent crime?

Did I say to be alone?
Well, that's really not the truth,
With the ever begging gulls who,
Poop upon your head . . . Uncouth?

The pelicans still skim the waves,
Bills holding more than their belly can,
With apologies to Ogden Nash,
But that rhyme was in my plan.

The porpoises are not deterred,
By the cold to take a swim,
Their bottle noses and fins arise,
As they feed at every whim.

The marshes turn from green to brown,
But remain an estuary,
Where life begins and thrives,
Be it June or February.

The sun shines not so awfully hot,
The bugs and crowds are gone.
Not many places to eat or shop,
Leaving we lovers quite alone.

Yes, Edisto at winter time,
I can hardly wait to go again,
Where God unrolls his scroll of blue,
Leaving no doubt its part of heaven.

Talent Persists!

My great friend Dick Buzard, whose father was a professional musician, gave me the following story about two of his father's peers.

It's a story, parable if you will, that has great meaning to me. It would be presumptuous of me to try to interpret it for you. Perhaps if you draw your own conclusions, you will be rewarded accordingly. The tale is as follows.

Meredith Wilson, the musical comedy composer, music man, etc., played *piccolo* in the famous **John Philip Sousa's** (The March King) band. In his autobiography, he tells the story of that band playing a special concert for a very wealthy king. It seems that the band played so beautifully and delighted the king to the point that he said, "Boys, your music gave me such pleasure that I want you to go to my counting house and fill your instruments with gold pieces."

Mr. Wilson said, "I can still visualize the activity of my fellow musicians as they poured the precious metal into their instruments. It created a great concerto as the solid gold trickled into the cavern of the giant *tuba* slithered down the neck of the *bassoon* and spilled over the bell of the *French horn,* and there I stood with my *piccolo.*"

The Thrill of Victory . . .
The Agony of . . . !

We were decided **underdogs** against **Bishop England High School**. Besides trying to make up for a mediocre season, our overwhelmingly **Protestant** School considered beating **those Catholics a crusade** worthy of any extra effort it might take to pull it off.

We slowed their high-powered offense to the point that, with less than two minutes left in the game, we still had a chance with the score being 12 to 7 in their favor.

Once again our defense held them to three downs and having to **punt** from their own 12-yard line. Hut 1 . . . hut 2 . . . the center hiked the ball to the punter. I broke through the line and the blocking back from my linebacker position just as he was kicking the ball. I not only blocked it but the ball stuck right in my stomach allowing me to breathlessly stumble over the goal line. **Touchdown?** . . . Thirteen to twelve our favor?

The crowd went crazy; the cheerleaders yelled, "Go back . . . Go back . . . Go back into the woods.

"You haven't got . . . you haven't got . . . you haven't got the goods. You haven't got the rhythm . . . you haven't got the Jazz . . .

"You haven't got the team St. Andrews has!"

But suddenly there was complete silence; everyone had been too busy jumping on me, carrying me around like a rag doll, and generally agreeing that I was the greatest to notice that infernal handkerchief, which stood out like a giant parachute as it floated in slow motion to the ground, off sides? Off sides? **Off sides?**

Fame is so fleeting!

Oh Do Now!

It was a typical "Lovely Weather for Ducks" morning at the rice field on Tommy Ravinel's plantation near Georgetown. The thin sheet of ice covering the tea-colored water crackled as the flat-bottomed boat polled by "Moses" transported us to the duck blind near the middle of the flooded acreage.

The sun peeping around the clouds on and above the horizon shone off the misty rain and sparkled on the ripples created by the movement of the bateau and the wind in the water. I had to muster much strength to quash the desire to break into song, "Oh what a Beautiful Morning" for fear of frightening the ducks and upsetting the boat with Moses' convulsive laughter.

Now I'm here to tell you—that Moses could laugh. At my any attempt at humor, his handsome, pure shiny black, character and weather-lined face would break into a wide grin and say, "Oh, do now, Mr. Bill." Then his massive muscular body would shake with a laughter that seemed to come all the way from the tip of his toes.

As soon as we got in, the blind three ducks got up way over the other side of the field. They were, in fact, so far away that Moses said, "Don't shoot. You'll scare the others." It was too late! I had already shot and one of those ducks fell into the water. "Mr. Bill, dats some real good shootin'. I ain't nebber seen no twelbe gage shoot so faa."

"Well, ya know, Moses, I hate to brag, but I can shoot pretty well."

"Yesh, sa, I certainly do see dat."

But alas that day, the duck population was in no further danger. In spite of the fact that ducks flew all around us, and I shot more than a box of shells, not another "feather was cut."

As we were rowing back to the levy, Moses broke the silence imposed by my pouting saying, "Hey, Mr. Bill, I ain't mean to mak ya mad."

"What is it, Moses?"

"I say, Mr. Bill, I ain't mean to mak ya mad but . . ."

"Go on, Moses, say what you got to say."

"Well, ya kno dat duck ya shoot."

"Yea, what about it?"

"Ain't no blood on 'em!"

"So what, Moses!"

"Well, Mr. Bill, I just haf to tell ya . . . I tink ya miss 'em so faa . . . he die laughin'!"

"Oh, do now, Moses!"

Mandy

As I held her in my arms with her black button nose snuggling into the crease of my elbow, I could feel her muscles tense trying to keep from breaking the spell by having to scratch that awful itch from which she has suffered the past few years. Rather than the sleek muscular body that was built from chasing squirrels, birds, and that half rubber ball she carried everywhere, the steroids that used to relieve the itching had now destroyed her kidneys and left her a blob of fluid.

I finally realized that not even her beloved stuffed dolphin, with which she had slept all of her life, could offer her comfort as most of the night I listened to thump of her leg and the whimper of pain coming from her bed by the vanity. That realization made the fateful decision that would finally end her discomfort a necessity.

After more than a dozen calls beginning at 6:30 a.m., I was finally able to ask the vet's receptionist for an appointment. June was still asleep, so I left her a note on the coffee pot, and Mandy and I left in the car. She loved to ride and was usually all over the car barking at other autos, joggers, and just everything she saw. But this morning, she lay quietly in my lap. Yes, I believe she lay there to allow for one last moment of a mutually requited love for which most mankind quests and of which few attain.

As we arrived at our destination, I thought I could get through this without embarrassing Mandy and me, but to be sure, I folded a $20 bill in my hand and intended to hand the lady the animal and the money and leave without comment as we had said our good-byes in the car. But just I as attempted to hand her to the receptionist, that infernal phone rang. While I waited for her to finish the call, a lady across the desk in the cat waiting room said, "What a beautiful little white dog." I just couldn't handle it any longer; the tears that I had privately shed for Mama, Daddy, Mr. Byrd, and "Big Mama" burst forth in public as uncontrolled sobbing. In a final sympathetic gesture, Mandy tenderly licked my cheek as if to say, "Its OK,

Goggy." The last thing she ever tasted was my salty tears of sadness, love, and memories.

If I am not in a position to make that "last decision" concerning quality of life or death, please do it for me without hesitation or trepidation. If you will, God will surely allow me to return (in some form) to kiss away your tears!

Hickory Dickory

A true tale of woe—or should that be a tail of woe—you be the judge!

It was our turn to host the three couples in our monthly bridge club. You'd never know that we'd been friends with these folks for many years the way my June had me cleaning windows, scrubbing floors, and polishing furniture. But they've only been out a couple of times since we moved here from the prestigious Timberlake Plantation. Timberlake is a place where if you had a big black bug that crawled up the wall at a most inappropriate time, you had a "palmetto bug," whereas our place is in the middle of 3 and ½ acres of pine trees, they are just plain roaches. But then that has not been a problem as we use all of the stuff that seems to keep the vermin and varmints under control.

Being all Methodists, happily married, and aged from sixty-five to eighty-five years, we are a compatible group who enjoys going out to supper, playing bridge, and swapping tales (some might call it gossiping) once a month. I still don't understand why all of the spit and polish, but then, I guess that's a female thing, and I'm not about to blow years of marriage over having to help clean up once in every four months. And then, I must admit the house did look pretty good.

Everything was going along very well until Puddles, our sixteen-year-old but still agile cat, decided that she was tired of watching TV in the bedroom and started squalling for us to let her meet our friends. I let her out since they do not seem to dislike cats and since she is a well behaved but very sociable animal who, after she greets everyone, usually returns to her sleeping place on our bed. We laughed as she showed off by bringing out her favorite toy for us to throw for her to attack or fetch. She was in top form until she abruptly decided that the show was over and left us to our cards.

Things were going right well as I made an extra trick or two and set a contract or two with the help of good partner communication until . . .

Hickory Dickory Dock
It was approaching nine o'clock.
As Puddles walked in with a mouse
That she let go right here in the house
With nary a care for the shock.

Hickory Dickory Exclaim
They lost all interest in the game.
Puddles felt no need to repent
As under the fridge Mousie went
It's the cat not me whose the blame.

Hickory Dickory Beware
Get that lady off the chair.
The husbands all laughed as they spy
Wives who've not been nearly so spry
For many and many a year.

Hickory Dickory Tee Hee
June thinks it's not so funnee,
To see all of our guests,
With knees up to their chests,
While Puddles struts proudly with glee.

Hickory Dickory Shazam,
Puddles made the only grand slam
While I'm accused of a renege
For destroying her fancy shindig
As to Puddles she gave not a damn.

Hickory Dickory Dock.
The mouse whose only ad hoc
Was to escape with his hide,
I've named him Clyde,
Hickory Dickory Dock!

Through the Woods

Our thanksgivings in the 1930s and 1940s began when Daddy got home from work on the Wednesday afternoon before thanksgiving. When he pulled in the driveway, the excitement began as we were waiting at the door to get into the car for the fifty-five-mile trip to my grandparent's house in Eutawville. Perhaps it was not "over the river," but it was a bumpy trip through the woods on the sandy "Old State Road" in our '35 Chevy (we did not have a sleigh).

Since Daddy saw no need for a car radio (if they were available at the time), we entertained ourselves by counting cows (you lost all your cows if you passed a cemetery on your side) and by reading the Burma Shave signs
(a man to win
a girl's applause
must act, not look
like Santa Claus.
Burma Shave!)

We arrived to find a festive atmosphere with Grandma, Granddaddy, Aunts, Uncles, younger cousins, and an assortment of neighbors and the neighborhood's ever-present dogs and cats waiting with open arms and wagging tails.

The days were getting short, so we had an early supper of fried fish, grits, collards, and corn bread. They liked to eat before the fragrance of the food had to compete with the smell of the kerosene lamps. After the meal, the men gathered of the front porch or around the pot-bellied stove in the living room (according to the weather) to smoke their "roll-your-owns," swop stories, and plan the next day's hunting trip.

The women gathered in the dining room where they loosened the ropes on the pulleys which held the quilting frame hanging high up in the ceiling over the large dining room table. While they quilted with the scraps of every shape and description, they (gasp) gossiped, discussed their health, and who was going through the change and other things of lady's interest.

We played quiet games on the floor because after supper, "children are to be seen but not heard." Then, just before bedtime, Uncle Manley sat at the old upright piano and began playing the familiar songs and hymns. At his first notes, the whole family gathered around in a spirit of oneness to sing of the happy times and a glorious future.

We knew that bedtime had arrived when the Mamas sent us kids out to the house at the end of the path so that we would not have to awaken them to use the pot under the bed during the night. While we were gone, they laid out the pallets since there were not enough beds for each of the little ones to have one. I was the oldest, so I would go for the choice location next to the living room stove.

The holiday began early as Granddaddy, not too quietly, brought in the wood to get the banked fires going so that the ladies could get started preparing the thanksgiving feast.

Then the men began gathering in the front yard preparing to leave for the morning bird hunt.

As they loaded the dogs in the back of the truck, they told me that I, as a ten-year-old, was too young to go with them. "Maybe next year!" I guess Granddaddy saw my disappointment (hang-dog look as he called it) and told the other men that he was "all stove up" and for them to go on without him and to, by the way, leave old "Rattler" home because the dog had to have his winter tonic. No sooner than they were out of sight, Granddaddy came out of the barn with a brand-new 410 shotgun, a canvas hunting coat, and a whole box of shells. He said, "I was gonna save this for Christmas, but Sears-Robuck delivered it early, and your Grandma and I didn't see any sense in it just sitting here. Put on your coat, grab your gun, get Rattler, and hop in the car. Off we went—the old man, a very old dog, and a proud ten-year-old—to the fields to find the much sought-after partridges."

It was a good day. Granddaddy moved better than I had ever seen him; Rattler was a well-trained young dog again, and I felt more grown up than I ever had before. There were birds all over the place, and we shot usually at the same time. As the birds fell, we put each of them in the back of my new jacket, which I wore home bearing the trophies of the day.

Meanwhile, the thanksgiving dinner of turkey, venison, pork, corn bread "dressing," giblet gravy, rice, several kinds of greens, home-canned pickles of every description, homemade bread, desserts of pumpkin pie, peach cobbler, blackberry pie, and more kinds of cakes than you can imagine was about ready to put on the table.

The other men were already back when we arrived home. Daddy was the first to meet us as he asked rather smugly, "Well, how did the great hunters do?"

I said, "We got twelve birds."

Daddy asked me, "And how many did you get?"

Granddaddy replied, "He got 'em all. I never even cut a feather!"

I thought, *Surely God'll forgive him for that white lie, as for the first time in my life, I counted my blessings and just how much for which I had to be thankful.*

Maladies

rushed out to see their doctors. In those days, before the perfection of many of the modern antibiotics, any streptococcus infection was greatly feared.

When she called that evening, I asked jokingly, "Well, will the office have to close down? How many cases of "the fever" did they discover?"

For this, she replied, "Only one ... *me!*"

Wilber and Sparky

I never thought much about *Alzheimer's* until I heard Mrs. Nancy Reagan's presentation at the Republican convention. It certainly put the disease in perspective as she discussed losing her beloved husband "a little bit at a time."

Thankfully, my encounters with the malady have been limited to some folks in the early stages of the regression and have, as a matter of fact, been somewhat tender. But before continuing with this anecdote, I must state emphatically that nothing I write should be construed as making light of or in any way understating the sorrows created by Alzheimer's! So now, with that understanding, let us get on with the story.

While returning home via our rural tar and gravel road rear Simpsonville, South Carolina, June, my wife, and I saw an old man and his cocker spaniel fall in the ditch. Fearing the worse, we traveled the one hundred or so yards separating us in record time. As I slid the auto to an abrupt halt, June was out in a flash to see what help they might need. However, before she could do anything, he got right up, still hanging on to the dog leash, and appeared to be in good shape. But in spite of his apparent healthy demeanor, a ride home seemed to be prudent. Their pleasure at being plucked out of the midday sun and into the comfort of our air-conditioned "Park Avenue" was obvious as the dog wagged his bobbed tail and the gentleman flashed, just a little wider, the smile that had never left his face.

"We're June and Bill, and who are you, sir?"

"How do you do, sir and madam? I'm Wilber Cleckly, and this is my dog Sparky," was his gallant reply.

"Someone must be concerned about you . . . just where do you live?"

He answered without hesitation, "I live with my daughter, Alice, at 323 Daley Ave."

I said to June, "See that peculiar red marking on Sparky's right ear . . . I know that dog. They must live nearby, but neither Alice nor Daley Avenue rings a bell."

"Mr. Cleckly, are you sure about that address?"

To that query, he just smiled and Sparky just wagged his tail.

After about a half hour of riding through some of the newer subdivisions and having no success in locating anything familiar, I decided to take them home with us and wait to see what would happen.

After seating them in our bright and cool "Charleston room," getting iced tea and cookies for Mr. "C," and a bowl of water and a dog cookie for his pal, they seemed to be comfortably settling down for an extended stay. Approaching frustration necessitated an increased vigilance in the search for a solution to this situation before having to call the police. So finally, recognizing his confusion, I did what I should have done much earlier and asked if he would allow me to look in his wallet for some identification. He did not object, so I was able to confirm that the information he gave us was indeed correct, *to a point*.

Written on the wallet ID card was—*in case of emergency*, contact Alice Wyman at 323 Daley Ave. *Chicago, Ill* . . . phone 313-555-3469.

We promptly called that number and, blessedly, got right through to Alice. She, with much concern, gave us the phone number of his other daughter, her sister, Ronda, who lived just a block behind us. In just a minute or two, a frantic but embarrassed, relieved, and grateful daughter was at our door to pick up "Daddy" and "Red Man." (Sparky was Alice's dog in Chicago.)

Most every day for the rest of his lengthy visit, we watched the happy old man and his contented canine companion as they passed our home on their daily stroll. Anytime I happened to be in the yard when they passed, we spoke, and he always said the same thing, "Hi, I'm Wilber, and who might you be?" Sparky (er . . . a . . . Red Man) just looked up at me, smiled, and wagged his tail.

The Greatest of These . . . !

This is the second of two anecdotes that I will write about dementia. Before I begin, it is important to me that the reader understands that I would never do anything to make light of anything about that disease. "Losing him a little lit at a time"—Mrs. Reagan's statement at the Republican convention made me (and I hope you) resolve to never return the Alzheimer's Association envelope empty again. With that in mind, let us continue.

George Blocker has some form of dementia, and Mrs. Blocker is on oxygen. But in spite of all of that, every time I stop by, they greet me with a smile and without complaint. The physical ailment of Mrs. Blocker is familiar, and I understand a little about them, but his condition is a mystery to me. George's eyes are so bright, his coloring is so good, and voice so strong that it is difficult to accept that he also is sick.

One day, last month, while driving him to his doctor's appointment, I attempted some idle conversation which went something like this: "What was your business before retirement?"

He thought for a minute and replied, "I really don't know!"

"How long have you and Mrs. B. been married?"

"Gosh, I just can't remember."

"You folks are obviously not from Columbia. Where did you come from?"

"I can't think of it right now!"

Though he never gave any answers, there was no frustration, just peaceful answers.

A few weeks later as we met again for me to give him a ride for his dentist appointment, I was running a little late. As usually happens when you're in a hurry, nothing seems to go right. On our way out of the living room, he had to stop by the sink to take his medicine. As we got out of the back door and down the two steps to the car port, he had to go back to get his hat. At the next attempt he made it to buckling himself into the front seat when he got very nervous, unbuckled, opened the door, and rushed back into the house. I hustled right behind him mumbling something about being sorry I was not on time but that he could at least try to help me make up the time so we wouldn't be late. But he paid me no mind. Something had forced its way through the veil that had been descending over his memory. As we entered the kitchen, he went over to his wife of sixty years, moved the oxygen tubes aside, and planted on her lips the biggest old *kiss* you ever saw. She just smiled as he said, "Bye now." With that done and without further ado, we were happily on our way just five minutes late.

I thought, *It must have taken something of extreme power to break through that curtain which increasingly separates the past from the immediate . . . just what could it have been?* As I meditated on the possible theorems, one sentence written over nineteen hundred years ago kept crossing my mind. It is a statement of such extreme strength and energy that anything else I have ever read on thought pales in comparison of significance.

St. Paul said it, and it's in the Bible. It goes like this: "And now abides faith, hope, love, these three; but the greatest of these is love!"

Grandchildren

Out of the Mouth's of Babes

Shortly, our children, **Richard** and **Barbie**, are going to have either (according to that new witchcraft machine) a little boy on a little girl with a large misplaced appendix.

Assuming that it is a male, they will name him **Richard** IV.

With such a distinguished name, what to call the little fellow is a problem. Since **Lucy** had "little" **Rickie,** the diminutive has become popular as a prefix to a baby's name—so we have to explore that possibility.

Little Richard might not be acceptable since it has been taken by a black singer with questionable sexual orientation. **Dickie** sounds like the fugitive from an unfinished shirt factory and **little dick** will haunt him the rest of his life as it insinuates a misstep in the circumcision procedure.

I think I'll just call him **Bubba!**

On a normal hot July day in our South Carolina Low Country, while camping in our tent, a first-class storm came up. **Barbie,** who was at that time about four years old, kept saying she had to go to the bathroom. It was impractical since the rain coming down in sheets was accompanied by blinding lightning and booming thunder.

She overcame her newly acquired modesty and, if we promised "not to look," would use the "pot" we had for that purpose. After getting it set up in the back of the tent, our attention returned to the tempest. As a matter of fact, I guess we forgot about her until we heard her *strained* little voice ask, "Anybody got any toilet paper!"

While playing her *first baseball game,* **Brittany** (my eight-year-old granddaughter) hit what was a possible *triple.* The coach encouraged her to round second base and run for third, but the throw was unusually good, and she was tagged *out* standing up. The coach—perhaps harsher than he intended—said, "Why didn't you slide?" With tears running down her cheeks and brushing off her little fanny Brittany said, "Girls don't slide!"

While on one of our bus trips with the grandchildren, an adult fellow traveler and I were discussing **Lewis Grizzard.** Because I am such a fan of his and have read everything he and anyone else has written about him, I have come to the conclusion that in spite of his talent and humor that the fame had spoiled him but not his writing.

I made the statement, "Grizzard was spoiled according to him and his last wife." I didn't know that *Ryan*, my ten-year-old grandson, was listening until he piped in saying, "He must have had grandparents like mine!" (Wow . . . what a complement!)

December 1995

(A letter to my four-month-old grandson)

Dear Rich,

It is Christmas. A time when folks think a lot about very special babies . . . yes, very special babies just like you!

We're so grateful that God has allowed us to be a part of your trip through eternity—from cherub, to prenatal, to baby, and hopefully we'll be allowed to witness at least some parts of your little boyhood, adolescence, and adulthood. Then, perhaps at some point in time, we can prove that there is something to this guardian angel stuff.

Though you and I belong to different denominations, we still belong to the same Church—the Church of Jesus Christ! Please remember that the two most powerful things in your life are, now and will forever be, your family and Jesus Christ (and his teachings, hopefully through his Church) Though it sounds somewhat cynical, believe me when I tell you that "when the chips are down," they are the only things on which you can always depend. Build on those relationships, nurture them, covet them, sacrifice for them, swallow your pride, and do everything within the remotest reason to make those two parts of your life work. If you do that, you will offer yourself a chance for a happy life!

While Church and family are most important, don't neglect to study the lives of people whom you most admire. A few of my heroes (actual and fictional) are: William Shakespeare, Julius Caesar, Don Quixote, King Arthur, the "Fathers of our Country" (especially Thomas Jefferson), Douglas MacArthur, Jefferson Davis, Richard Nixon (despite his faults), and St. Francis of Assisi. I'm giving you a copy of St. Francis's prayer (in bookmark), a rosary (in a container), and a statue of him. All of this is to encourage you to study the life of this man, who loved God, people, animals, nature, and is

Though the greatly outnumbered *Rebel's* fighting skill caused great casualties among the Northerners, the *Yankees* just kept on coming. As the number of Southern soldiers declined and more blue clad reserves came over the hill, it became apparent that the rebel cause was all but lost.

Just imagine the consternation of this super southern patriot "Goggy" as he heard his five-year-old grandson, *Thomas,* say to his three-week-old cousin, "Adam, there are just too many of them. We can't win . . . . Don't you think we had better start rooting for the Yankees!"

Odds and Ends

Beth and Adam brought us a box of candy that tastes just like **Heath Bars**. June has done a wonderful job of losing the weight she has been concerned about. I caught her eating two bars of that candy. She has no will power. I ate the remaining thirteen bars while she took her nap. Oh, how we husbands sacrifice for our wives!

Did you ever wonder why?

We drive on parkways and park on driveways!

If pantie is singular, why isn't brassiere plural?

If olive oil comes from olives, where does baby oil come from?

To begin the **children's sermon** at church, **Preacher John Hipp** inquired of the children, "What's the first think that you think of when you think of Church?"

Doctor Douglas's seven-year-old brought the congregation down with laughter when he replied, "Boring!"

If you're not **living on the edge**, you've got **too much room!**

Why do **Columbia** folks say, "Where are the grits? They **are** on the table."

While Charleston natives say, "Where **is** the grits? It **is** on the table." Is **grits** a bunch of ground corn grains or a single semiliquid dish?

When someone or something acted silly, **my daddy** would often say, "He must be Ma'shugie!" I think the word came from the Jewish word **Mashuga** (spelling?) meaning crazy.

It has not been so long since **washday** included the following equipment: a clothesline, clothespins, and a clothesline pole to hold the wet clothes weighted line up off the ground. Additional equipment included a wood pile, a rock lined fire pit, big black wash pot, homemade lye soap, and a bleached white paddle to stir the clothes in the boiling water. A strong back for lifting and powerful hands for wringing were also helpful.

On March 14, 1996, I wrote Chapin Mayor Stan Shealy a **postal card** which said:

Just Fishin'

A boy, his dad and a bamboo pole
A headin' out to their favorite fishin' hole.
Now what could be more peaceful than that
A man, his son, and a floppy hat.
Inviting the sun to find some space
In an already covered freckled face.
They talked of things which could change his life
By making a man of peace without much strife.
More than Alice's shoes and ships and sealing wax
But most of all we were together just to relax.
Relax you say as the cork was pulled down
By a bream which weighed nearly a pound.
I think that's a keeper my daddy explained
Well, it's bigger than yours I quickly exclaimed.
"Dad, I've been thinkin' about becoming a man
I want to be like you if only I can."
"What do you think will help me to grow
To be loving and tough and learn all that you know?"
"Now, Billy, I thank you for what you say
And you must know that it took more than just a day.
To learn the best way to live and be really alive
Worshiping God, loving your Mom and all that jive.
I once read a poem called *The Road Less Traveled*
Go your own way though it's not paved but graveled.
If you only go the ways of the world
You'll find many an oyster but rarely a pearl.
Now I'm an old man with grandsons of my own
And I remember those days which have long ago gone.
When the first one was ten I bought him a pole
And we went fishing where many tales we told.
And he rubbed it in when he got the biggest fish
And that answered my prayers and my every wish.

Then he said, "Goggy, what's it like being a man?"
I said, "I'll explain it to you the best that I can."
"You see my daddy and I fished this same hole
And the wonders of life were the stories he told.
The best thing he said that I hope you will learn
Is "Just to Love and be Loved in Return."
The time's rapidly approaching when I'll meet him again
When we'll greet each other with a hug and a grin.
And immediately head to the celestial pond
Where we'll renew our interrupted bond.
We'll look down below as eternity's only begun
See you and your siblings and a job well done.

Grandma's Country Yard

I learned about the birds and bees in Grandma's country yard,
No, not the kind in the loft of the barn,
With the neighbor's daughter without regard,
For the boys in town who would spin the yarn.
Nothing like that at my grandma's country house,
Where the cardinals and blue jays light in the trees,
And if you sat like a quiet little mouse,
You could hear the oak leaves sing in the breeze.
The path to the house with the cut out C,
Was lined with strawberry plants galore,
So you sat, ate berries, and felt carefree,
And hoped no one would open the door.
Listen to ole Rattler just scratching his fleas,
Under the steps in the cool damp sand,
And you can tinkle wherever you please,
'Cause this is desolate country in Dixie land.
Camellias and azaleas reach to the sky and beget,
Images of wars, battles, and strife,
With pirates in the bushes with Spanish bayonet,
And Oleander leaves for sword and knife,
Memories of those are beyond compare,
I'll not ever forget as it comes so seldom,
Because so often people are afraid to share,
Those emotions that offer the healing balm.
In a resting place in the land of the pine,
Near The Great Santee by The old Churchyard,
Lies Grandma and Granddaddy since Sixty Nine,
But it was just yesterday that we loved . . .
in Grandma's country yard.

I think it was a September evening in 1943, that *Mama* and I went to the *Gloria Theater* in downtown Charleston to see, the now classic motion picture, *Casablanca*.

As we left the theater, we could not help but become a part of the excitement created by the *Newspaper Boys* shouting, "Extra . . . extra . . . read all about it . . . Italy surrenders to the allies."

There was dancing, shouting, and crying by many, but that lady was hugging her little girl and sobbing. "He's comin' home . . . he's coming home." This made an extreme impression and put a prayer in the psyche of this eleven-year-old that has never been forgotten. *Please, God. Don't let war happen again!* Though we have since fought in *Korea, Vietnam, Granada, Desert Storm,* and others, that prayer is as fervent as ever, but *it* has become the more mature supplication of *please, God, peace with honor!*

Folks from the *North* call 'em *red potatoes*; we call 'em *new potatoes*.

Folks north of *Orangeburg* call them *chiggers*; we call them *red bugs*.

Rich *Yankees* call 'em *sweetbreads*; we call them sheep guts.

Yankees call them *hog guts*; we call 'em *chitlins*.

We call them *soft drinks, cokes, or dopes; Yankees* say *soda*.

A *parable* is an earthly story with a heavenly meaning.

I made some *bagels* with my new bread machine. They were not so good. As a matter of fact, *they were so heavy*. How heavy were they? Well, they were so heavy that I threw them out in the lake to the ducks, and a duck ate one and sank to the bottom. Ta daaa!

Vacations at Granddaddy's and Grandmama's

(With apologies to Herman Hupfeld, Dooley Wilson and Casablanca.)

This day and age we're living in give cause for apprehension. With speed and new invention and things like fourth dimension, and no matter what the progress or what may yet be proved, the simple facts of life are such that they cannot be removed!

A quick leap from under the pile of quilts in that unheated bedroom with the window open, regardless of the outside temperature, created a sudden wide awakening welcome to a new day. It was a necessary quickly acquired skill to jump right into your clothes, at least as fast as could a present-day fireman.

Though I was only at my country grandparent's Eutawville, South Carolina, home on weekends and much of the summer, when there, I, as the oldest grandchild, had certain tasks. The one which I liked the least was to collect the pots from under the beds and take them to dump into the little house with the crescent on the door out back. It was disgusting and very cold, but when I complained Granddaddy's words of wisdom "Billy, it'll make you tough" didn't make it any warmer smell any sweeter, nor the path any shorter.

However, my saving grace was the warm kitchen with the great woodstove, which after being banked for the night, was stoked into a blazing inferno to make the coffee "hot water tea" that was a mixture of hot water, real cream, and lots of sugar in a cup stuffed with bread, which I drank 'cause coffee will make you turn "black," grits that had been simmering and stirred several times during the night, scrambled eggs fresh from just under the hens, fried partridge from the iron frying pan that was never washed because it was "seasoned," and great cat head biscuits.

As an aside, biscuits seemed to have had a certain mystique in our family as the story was often told of my great-grandma dying in that same kitchen over that same stove with biscuit dough on her hands.

After breakfast during the week, Granddaddy and I would get his carpenter tools together and go off to the jobsite where the rest of his crew met him, and we worked building houses. It didn't seem to bother him to build a large ornate house for someone else while living in just an adequate plain old country home.

We worked hard, ate our luncheon feast of pork or fish sandwiches, and took a half-hour rest under a shade tree before continuing the tasks at hand. It was not necessary to take water if we were working by a fast-moving stream. In that case, we had two dippers (sometimes enamel and sometimes gourds). One was on one tree for the white workers, and the other was on another tree for the blacks. Discrimination? Both dippers dipped out of the same stream and were identical. But then that's a subject for another day.

On Saturdays, we left before breakfast, got the dogs and our shotguns, and went bird hunting. Watching those dogs work the fields and suddenly go into a ridged point was the beginning of a thrilling series of events. Granddaddy was in complete control of the situation. "Easy now, Rattler . . . don't flush that covey too soon for us to get a good shot . . . the dog, and as a matter of fact, I obeyed as we quivered all with nervous anticipation of the impending drama of ten or more birds rising as one with the noise like a rushing wind. Then the thunder of Gann's automatic 12-gauge's three quick shots and my one created the end of the drama. It was over except for the soft-mouthed dogs proudly picking up without further damage to the fallen birds and proudly dropping them at his feet."

The rest of the day was spent running errands. The preverbal general store with the town philosophers gathered around the potbellied stove was, of course, always the highlight of the trip. Gran proudly showed me off to the group. But that was the extent of my involvement as I knew that I was to listen and to be seen but not heard.

The evenings were usually a quiet time with an occasional family story told by Grandma or some uncle or aunt. Gran rarely entered into that part of family interaction because he was intent of listening through the static to the Louisiana Hayride or the Grand Ole Opry starring Little Jimmy Dickens.

It soon became bedtime, and if it was a bath day, the pecking order was enforced and the oldest got to use the tub of hot water by the kitchen stove first. I was, of course, last but the used water still washed clean. I think that scrubbing with the homemade lye soap killed all the germs deposited by the previous bathers.

It was a time of callused hands, turpentine for healing, caster oil as a preventative and Lydia Pinkham's for hot flashes. Yes, it was a time of, Sunday Church as a special time, honoring the old folks, of "Love thy neighbor," of getting half the town in the back of my daddy's flatbed truck for the five-mile trip to Eutawville Springs and pick up baseball games.

Oh, how I remember this as if it was yesterday. It's still the same old story *as time goes by!* Sigh, *as time goes by!*

Simple Times

Back in the 1940s and 1950s, even though the advertising was somewhat simpler, it was no less creative. A good example of that is **Burma Shave** shaving cream.

There were no super highways back then and all of the traveling was done on two-lane roads. The major ones were paved with a 55 mph speed limit and the secondary ones were mostly unpaved hard pack, muddy when wet and/or sandy. This gave more time for reading billboards and other signs along the way.

Burma Shave's message was on five red signs with white letters about one-foot-high-by-two-feet-long and spaced about one hundred feet apart. Each sign had part of the message painted on it. There were a lot of different messages on the signs, so finding one you had never seen was a game we played.

The only one I remember was on *the old State road* near Eutawville, and it went like this:

First sign—*a man to win*
Second sign—*a girl's applause*
Third sign—*must act, not look*
Fourth sign—*like Santa Claus*
Fifth sign—*Burma Shave!*

Grantland Rice, the great sports writer of the first half of the century, once said, "It matters not whether you win or lose, it's how you played the game."

Someone, not nearly as profound (I think it was me) said, "If you play the game right, you'll win most every time!"

As a child, I liked to try to play an *ocarina. What is that, you say? Well,* it is a small musical instrument made of terra-cotta shaped like a sweet potato (it was sometimes called a sweet potato) with a hole you blew into and had finger holes to create the different notes.

We'll awake to a stove which Santa Claus, Granddaddy or somebody had stoked to its glowing red hot best. The first thing we'll see when we wake up will be a candle-decorated pine sapling surrounded by St. Nick's generosity—fruit, nuts, candy, plus, on a good year, a bicycle, electric train, or scooter.

"What was that you said, Daddy . . . hunting?"

"Yea, let's go shoot some birds . . . Uncle Herbert said that we could come on over to his place. He said that he jumped four or five coveys just yesterday."

"Granddaddy, can we ride with you?"

"Oh yes, sir . . . I'll get the dogs in the back of the car. While I'm doin' that would you please get me my new 410 and some shells . . . lots of shells."

"Here, Rattler . . . here, Maude . . . git en dis car . . . we gonna git Grandma some partridge for supper tonight."

"Bye, Grandma, . . . bye Granddaddy . . . I love you . . . Merry Christmas . . . thank you . . . please come see us . . . what was that? A hug? . . . Oh yes, Ma'am." We can't miss that best present of all, being almost smothered in the massive bosom of the best Grandma in the whole wide world.

To paraphrase Mr. Dickens, God blessed us every one and may God bless you!

Merry Christmas!

Uncle Leon, Granddaddy's brother, lived with him, and Grandma for quite a few of Uncle Leon's last years. They, in fact, closed in the back porch to accommodate him. I don't think he had even been married, and I know that he was at least "one slab of ribs short of a barbecue dinner." I don't know his problem, but I do know every time June and I went by to visit Granddaddy almost had to whip him to make him keep his hands off June. When Leon was around, conversation was almost impossible with his constant interruptions. Had there been an attic in the house, I'm not sure anyone would see him.

In spite of the fact that Uncle Leon got on Granddaddy's nerves, his "sense of family" made him very kind to Uncle Leon.

Uncle Leon finally died and was buried in the family plot on the sand hill under the one-hundred-year-old oak tree that had for generations shaded the graves from the tropical Orangeburg County sun. In less than a year, the oak tree died!

The only, even slightly profane, thing I ever heard my *granddaddy* say was, "He drove me crazy all of his life, and now the *old bastard* killed my tree!

I *swear* was not acceptable verbiage for ladies and young kids. If I ever slipped up, *Mama* would not hesitate to say, "Billy, don't swear . . . *swanee!*" "I swanee" was just fine in any company, by anyone and in any situation.

I'm not saying that Mama wanted a little girl, but she dressed me in velvet and silk suits and spelled my name *Billie*. At about three years old, I remember the raucous when Daddy and Harold put a stop to that!

The *Tories* that live in the mid and upper state areas call it a red bud tree. We, Low Country folks, call it a Judas tree. You will recognize it as the first "red buds" in the spring time forest.

According to my Grandma, the reason for the insulting name is as follows: The legend of the *dogwood tree* is that because *Jesus's cross* was made of *dogwood* that the blooms of the tree would be pure white, in the shape of a cross, have a touch of red to signify *his* blood, have notches in the petals to show where the nails entered his body and would be the first blooms of spring.

The Red Bud Tree broke the code that all the other trees followed in allowing the dogwood to be the first to bloom. So the Red Bud's betrayal of the tree designed to carry our Lord into the fulfillment of the prophecies earned it the name of Christ's betrayer—Judas!

I heard a fundamentalist *radio preacher* sermonizing about, "The devil's in the phone booth dialin' 911, 'cause the Church is on its knees loading up their gun!"

Picture a housewife sitting in front of the TV, a book in her hand, papers strewn everywhere, a beer on the side table, and a cigarette hanging out of her mouth.

As her husband entered the front door, she asked, "How was your visit to the *doctor?*"

To this, the husband replied, "He said my heart is good, my blood pressure is fine, and my cholesterol is OK, but that I could use some clean underwear!"

If you live in the fast lane, it's very probable that you'll get to the end of the road *much too fast!*

Would a HERmit be a hermit if she had a HEmit with whom to share a life?

My daddy cut down our beautiful—producing—*Japanese persimmon tree* on December 8, 1941! Why? Think about it you students of history!

When served *cornflakes* for breakfast, *my daddy* crushed them with his hand in order to get more in his *cereal bowl*. This was to the accompaniment of *Mama's*, "Oh, Bill, that is so tacky!"

If I kissed two girls with *mono*, would I get *stereo?*

I heard of a new organization called *DAM*. It stands for *mothers against dyslexia!* Get it? Think about it.

While perusing the records of the 1932-*medical records* in *Charleston*, I was included as being among the first to have received *microsurgery*. Unfortunately, it was my *circumcision!*

My *daddy* said that he never bet again after losing 50¢ to a man who bet him that he could remove Daddy's vest without taking off Daddy's coat first!

If she happened to see me walking abound with a pout on my face, Grandma Shingler would often ask, "Now who licked the *red off your candy?*"

Family Cussin' and Other
One Liners

Note: Anytime I use unusual spelling in the dialog, I am not making fun of their grammar because they were conscientious in their efforts to be grammatically correct. I am simply trying to indicate a geechee or Orangeburg County dialect.

My mama's cuss words were, to the best of my knowledge, nonexistent or at least very limited. The vilest one that I remember as her favorite was *Crime-o-nent-ly!* It was used as an expression of aggravation such as, "*Crimeonently*, Billy, why didn't you wipe your feet when you came in from the chicken yard?"

"I *swanny*" was an expression of astonishment. For example, "You passed Latin three months in a row . . . well, I *swanny*."

I never heard Daddy use anything worse than *John brown it.*

One day, we were returning from a trip to Grandma Bowen's house across the Ashley River. On the way home, the bridge opened to let a ship come through, and Daddy thought it would be a good idea to get out and see the ship. Just as he opened his door, a city bus came by and took the door right out of his hand. Miraculously, he was not physically hurt. All he did was to sit down on the car seat and say, "John Brown it, Billy, that was a stupid thing to do!"

My granddaddy was a carpenter, as was his father before him. He built the first building that housed the Baptist Church in Eutawville. Granddaddy built the next two replacements plus the Methodist Church.

I stayed with them several summers and helped on his carpentry crew. In those days, it was all-hand tools. My job was sifting the sand through a screen to make the mortar for the brick masons.

Since we didn't have TV, story telling was a favorite form of entertainment. One evening, I was complaining about how hard the work was when **Granddaddy** said, "Ya gotta be tough, Billy. See dis scar on my fingga" (showing me his left index finger)

"Yes, sir, I see it."

"Well, one day, I was choppin' some wood stakes, and I chopped off dat fingga just above the knuckle. See huuh. Well, I picked up dat end and dipped it in some turpentine. I den dipped what was left of my fingga in it . . . then . . . I *chugged* dem back together, tied 'em wid a rag, and day grew back jus lak new." There it was. What can you say?

Obviously preparing for a date, June's brother, whom we called **brother**, came walking into the living room all dressed and smelling like he had just left the Old Spice factory. "Grand"—June's daddy—said, "come here, Brother, and let me pee in your pocket so you'll smell like a man!"

Early in my life, **Mama** recognized a part of my nature what came to be my most notable trait—that of being impatient and high strung. In that regard, she was constantly quoting the following little poem to me:

Little drops of water
Little grains of sand
Make a mighty ocean
and a mighty land.

That didn't work so well but, I believe, another she quoted did sink in . . .

When a job is once begun
Never quit till it is done.

It was not unusual for **Daddy** to say, "Come on, Billy, let's go down to Mr. Limehouse's store and get a dope." A dope was a Coca Cola. Oftentimes you got a penny bag of salted peanuts and poured in the bottle before you drank it. The salt made the "Coke" fizz up and the peanuts tasted so good. The trick is to keep some of the nuts in the bottle with your tongue while you got some of the liquid. Try it, I bet you'll like it. (As a matter of useless information, the reason Cokes were called dopes is that when it was originally formulated in Atlanta, it was made as a medicine and contained cocaine.)

Uncle Harold, my mama's brother, was quite a character and was my daddy's very good friend. Hunting and fishing was his, as it was my **daddy's**, first love. One night, when I was three or less, **Mama** said, "Kiss your daddy good night."

Uncle Harold said, "Big guys don't kiss guys!" For better or for worse, I don't think I ever kissed my daddy again.

Mama's Driving

My mama, Clarine Bowen, never learned to drive until after Daddy died, which would have made her in her early sixties. When Daddy left us, Mama lived alone and was still working, so she had to depend on others for transportation. Always having been pretty independent, she felt the need to control her own destiny behind the wheel of the car, so she took driving lessons.

I have no idea about the trials and tribulations of the driving instructor and the license examiner, but I do know that the few times when Daddy, from whom I inherited my total lack of patience, tried to teach Mama to drive, the experience turned into a shouting match.

The one time that really stands out was on the way back down the *Old State Road* from Eutawville to Goose Creek. That road was not paved. When dry, keeping the front wheels in the ruts of the sand surface made for a smoother ride. When it was wet, just keeping the car from sliding off the road into the ditch required the skill of a "stock car driver." "Keep it in the ruts, Bill" was Mama's constant reminder to Daddy, the driver.

In a weak moment, after much cajoling by Mama, Daddy finally gave in, with a "keep it in the ruts, Clarine," and let her try to drive.

With much scraping of first through third gears, we were rolling along quite nicely until we came to the large country Free Will Baptist Church, near Aunt Eva's place, where they were having a funeral. The *hearse* had just arrived and was parked in the road getting prepared for the pallbearers to take the body into the church.

Mama was bound to "keep it in the ruts" at all costs. I swear to you, she ran right into the back of that big black car sending pallbearers (in spite of the fact they were in their "Sunday Best") diving for the side of the road.

As a nine-year-old, I was not informed about how Daddy handled the situation, but I do know there was much weeping and wailing during the conversation that preceded our getaway.

Reaching for the anchor rope to pull in that useless piece of metal, I found the line still coiled under the bow cap. What in the world is going on? Oh my goodness! I forgot to tie on that brand-new "borrowed" *boat brake!*

It was a long trip home!

June (My Island Girl)

That's Life

Just a pat on the head when you're in the mood,
I'll do what you want no matter the strife,
Says Molly the dog, for just a little food,
I'll lick your hand and love you forever . . . that's my life!

Stroke my fur and pat my head, but only when I say,
My entrance is so regal where are the drum and the fife,
Puddles' litter box has only the finest of clay,
Accept my love only on my cat terms . . . that's my life!

A time of electronics, sports, and DVDs,
Rocks, seashells, acorns, and an old pocketknife,
Make a boy child curious of all he sees,
Fantasies of adventure in distant lands . . . that's his life!

Mama's make up, old dresses, and hats,
Barbie dolls, stuffed animals, adventures of rife,
Make a girl child happy and often begats,
A fuzzy feeling, a hug, and a smile . . . That's her life!

Patience of Job and love like the Madonna,
A parent to the kids and the romance as a wife,
Gets it all done and rarely manana,
Hides her light under a bushel; so there . . . that's her life!

He tries to be macho and sometimes is gruff,
And would rather his recliner to Mom's Duncan Phyfe,
But Dad's an old softy who his toughness will bluff,
'Till a tear or a smile turns his firmness to mush . . . That's his life!

We have faith that God takes care of us all
While hoping we're complete living a life full of lithe
And love is the greatest and according to St. Paul.
As faith, hope, and love abide . . . We learn, truly that's life!

We Love Her Cookin'!

My wife, June, is a very good cook! At least I've not had any problem maintaining my 210-plus pounds while subsisting on her fare. As a matter of fact, I've enjoyed almost every meal. Well, at least until just recently, when she started fooling around with strange receipts and food varieties trying to cut down on the fat and salt content. It's a conspiracy by the fascist, communistic, and liberal left who made up those reports of the harmful effects of salt and fat. They took away my cigarettes! What comes next?—coffee, Butterfinger candy bars, cookies and milk at midnight, and salt and fat!? And who would ever believe that my beloved June would become an accomplice!

But alas I digress.

In spite of my opinion that she is a great food preparer, she seems to have problems at covered-dish suppers. We almost always bring back home at least half of what she prepared for the meal. It has gotten so bad that she doesn't put her name on the dish, sneaks it in paper bags, and never uses the same container twice. In spite of her attempts to keep people from knowing what particular concoction she brought, nothing has changed. We have lots of leftovers, and the cat eats pretty well. Trying to relieve her frustration and, perhaps selfishly, trying to keep from having to eat reheated victuals, I suggested that she just prepare casseroles, freeze what is left, and keep bringing it back until they eat it all. My suggestions didn't seem to help very much as they just fell on deaf ears.

It is just so difficult to understand—the food really is quite tasty and looks pretty good too. It must be like poi which the Hawaiians devoured like ambrosia, and I thought tasted like wallpaper paste. I guess the cliché fits—it's just what you're used to.

One time, to see if something different would help, she baked a pound cake. It was prepared just as her mother (who made the best cakes in the world) would have done. She carefully mixed the traditional pound of flour, butter, sugar, and all and baked it to a beautiful golden brown.

With such meticulous preparation, you'd think that it would have jumped off the serving plate, but I'm not kidding when I tell you that, except for being sliced, we brought it home just as we took it, not one piece was missing. These Methodist are so persnickety, I guess we'll have to join the Baptist Church, they'll eat anything. I felt so sorry for her that, as soon as we walked in the door, I took out a slice in order to make a dramatic show of enjoying it. Can you imagine our consternation when we discovered that someone had already removed that slice, taken a bite off the bottom, and put it right back in the cake! *Gasp*—what can I say?

On Easter Sunday, I asked *Nana* (June) if she had any special memories. She replied, "Yes, I certainly do. It was the year that my aunt Kary came to see us on Easter."

The Bunny was very good to Birdie, brother and me that year, and I really loved my basket with all of its ribbons and bows. It must have been especially beautiful as Aunt Kary "made over it" quite a lot.

I'll never forget those fateful words when *Mama* said, "Kary, you just take that basket home with you. I'll get June another one just like it."

Since it was totally unlike her, I think she just forgot. I never did get my basket!

June said that she was so tired. *How tired was she?* Well, she said that she was so tired that she moved the bathroom scale in front of the commode so that she could *weigh sitting down*! Taa daa—there's that darn drum again!

I heard a young person, who was trying to explain his lack of morals and self-discipline, say, "But times have changed!"

If I ever get to preach a sermon, it will be entitled, and, I hope, convince someone that, *times don't change, people do!*

Folks from other parts of our country call it a *patio* or *lanai*. We *Charlestonians* call it a *pe-a-zza!*

Isn't it strange that we, who are the inventors of disposable lifestyles, hesitate to dispose of anything?

Why do we hate to throw away?—burned-out BIC lighters, dead flashlight batteries, plastic Suebee "honey bear" containers, worn-out shoes, shorts, slacks, or pants that are two inches too small in the waist, out-of-style ties, empty razor blade holders or dull disposable razors, empty spray bottles, ragged belts, and jars.

Remember the disposable *double-edged razor blades* that you got rid of by sticking them in the hole in the back of the bathroom cabinet.

Why did the *chicken* cross the road?

To show the 'possum it could be done! Taa da!

Coach Brad Scott of the Clemson Tigers said that after fifteen years of marriage, he demanded his wife that she start preparing hot breakfasts for him.

Sure enough, the next morning, he got up and his *cornflakes* were on fire! (Where's that drum roll when I need it?)

In my pile of stuff, which June calls Junk, I found the old mayonnaise maker which, as I remembered, made the best I've ever tasted. "They don't make it like they used to." Yep, as was said at the beginning of *The Lone Ranger* radio show, "Let us return to the golden days of yesteryear." The maker is a glass jar which has a cover with a hold in it through which passes a dasher that you operate up and down as you would a butter churn. In the jar, you start with an egg, some lemon juice, mustard, sugar, and pepper. Through hole in the cover is added the oil while dashing aggressively.

The result is a creamy mayo-looking product that when spread on bread with vine-ripened-Low Country tomatoes tastes like wonderful tomatoes spread with used motor oil, especially when compared to present-day Hellman's Real Mayonnaise.

Kinda reminds you of concepts of and the actualities of senior citizen *sex* when compared to *the good ole days*.

Folks from the *North* call 'em *red potatoes*; we call 'em *new potatoes*.

Folks north of *Orangeburg* call them *chiggers*; we call them *red bugs*.

Rich *Yankees* call 'em sweetbreads; we call them sheep guts.

Yankees call them *hog guts*; we call 'em *chitlins*.

*W*e call them *soft drinks, cokes, or dopes*; *Yankees* say *soda*.

I have a theory why the *South* has so may beautiful women.

After the *war between the States* the carpetbaggers, and during World Wars I and II, the many *Yankees,* who moved down to work in our military bases and defense plants, married most of our "leftovers."

Our ugly women, who have so much more to offer than the best of their northern sisters, were taken home by the Yankees in droves leaving us to breed with the beauties that were left *producing only lovely southern belles!*

Be Yourself, Sweetheart

"Do what? Pick up what for what kind of pie?"

She repeated herself, "While you're in town, how about picking up a pound of whole pe*cons* so that I can make a pe*con pie for Barbie" (our baby who just had her first child)*.

"It's pe*can* . . . pe*can* . . . pe*can* pie! What the heck are you gonna do while you're cooking the pie . . . drink a soda?" I say while popping the lid on a RC Cola.

"I fly the *first flag of the confederacy*, own and have committed to memory every book and tape *Lewis Grizzard* ever produced, brag constantly about your family's cotton plantation, and am proud of our *southern heritage* almost to a fault and the first *Yankee* to move in the neighborhood has you talking just like 'em. The next thing . . . we'll be having cream-of-wheat and scrapple instead of *grits* and bacon for breakfast!"

I stood a little taller as I knew I had won when she said, "You are absolutely right. I just didn't realize what I was saying and will certainly not let that happen again! With that settled, would you please pick up some pe*cans* while you're out."

I was so proud as I replied, "That sounds much better, of course, I will . . . Sweetheart!"

Then I was stopped short in my tracks at her next request "When you past the *frig*, will you please hand me a *can of pop!*"

After having had *my breastbone* cut in half during heart surgery, I was depressed. Trying to cheer me up, the *doctor said*, "Don't be upset. I'll have you *playing good golf* in just a few months."

My reply was, "If that is the case, then I have seven or eight buddies who'll *sign up for the procedure*. I'm a terrible golfer."

We were anxious to get to *Edisto* to explore the dunes, the gullies, and the washes on the beaches and the bodies of two ex-smokers who had collectively gained fifty pounds.

We were amazed at what we found!

Without memory, we must experience everything for the first time—learning would be impossible, education would be meaningless, and relationships would have no value.

Jane and Elaine are *sisters*. Jane, after having moved to another city, came back home. Returning to town meant having to get a hairdresser; a dentist, and a doctor.

While being *examined by the ob-gyn* that Elaine had recommended the doctor decided that small talk was in order. Just as he was looking down under the sheet, her heart skipped a beat when he said, "It is certainly easy to tell you and Elaine are sisters"—pause—"Your voices sound just alike." Whew!

Foster Brooks, the *"drunken comedian,"* tells the story about the time he was pulled by the cops for driving while drunk. The magistrate said, "You're so drunk. You can't see."

"Not guilty," said Brooks, "I can see that *one-eyed cat* coming in the door."

To this, the judge replied, "That's a two eyed cat going out the door . . . guilty as charged!"

"I told you I knew him!"

While on a business trip to New York City, June, my wife, and I decided to take a few hours to do the tourist thing of checking out the sites and the people. I guess we were typical visitors with hurting necks from gawking at the massive building *ten times* higher than any we have in South Carolina. As we walked, I thought, *It is no wonder that the folks who live and work on these streets seem so intense, grumpy, and sad, after all, they see the sunshine only a few minutes a day in those cement canyons.* Though we never found the rudeness that is so often reported, we did, however, find a general indifference that was alien to our Palmetto State naivety.

Tiring of the drabness of the Wall Street area, we sauntered over to the more lively and open Rockefeller Plaza area and entered into the holiday card atmosphere created by the giant Christmas tree and the ice-skaters gliding gracefully over the ivory-like frozen liquid. The Yuletide mood was broken as I heard June say, "Why hello there . . . it's so good to see you. What are you doing so far north?"

To this, the person replied, "Thank you . . . it's nice to see you also. I'm here on business . . . and you are here for?"

"Business and pleasure."

"How nice . . . Bye now . . . have a safe trip home!"

"You too . . . Bye"!

June then turned to me and said, "I can't believe I don't remember that man's name . . . He is such a nice person who always speaks when I see him at the tennis courts . . . What in the world is his name? . . . Do you know?"

"Yes, I think so, and I don't believe that he lives in South Carolina nor plays at our courts. His face is familiar because you see it on TV almost every evening . . . His name is *Walter Cronkite!*"

"Gasp!"

Free Verse Glory

I hear the thunder,
Music from the sky,
That precludes the rain and hail,
Which nourishes the earth,
With nitrogen for food and ozone to refresh.

Soft droplets from above,
Showering us with velvet massage,
And puddles into water ribbons,
Flowing to the sea as rivers and as streams,
Creating estuaries nourished by the oceans and the bays.

Here live the lower orders,
Which feeds the invertebrate, bird, and mammal,
Who glorify the Lord,
With praises of adoration,
While others curse his name.

Praise him—praise him here on earth,
While cherubim and seraphim worship him in heaven.
Hear the thunder and see the lightning,
Lead me to his presence,
His glory out shines the sharpest bolt!

Glory . . . glory to his name!

Throw That Rock!

My dearest pastor friend Bill Williams declares (preachers don't swear, they declare or affirm) that this story is true.

A small Methodist Church in rural South Carolina still used the Board of Stewarts method of church government. After a great deal of pressure on them from the Women's Missionary Society, John Black, a member who owned the local liquor store, was brought before them for "church trial." The charges were *selling booze*, and if convicted, the sentence would be "expulsion" from the church's membership rolls!

John took his trial very seriously and used as his defense a biblical reference that seemed perfect before this *jury* that contained several of his very good customers. That scripture came from John 8:7—Let him, who is without sin, cast the first stone . . . !

The verdict was quick, decisive, and nearly unanimous. The next day in the window of *John Black's package store*, there appeared a large printed sign that said, NOT GUILTY!

The Road to Edisto and Paradise

Like charismatic parishioners,
Reaching for their God,
The arms of the great live oaks,
Create a shaded boulevard,

Spanish moss colored, a mystic Paine's gray,
That moves with every whim of breeze,
With rhythms the occult to emulate,
A dance their false gods for to please.

The narrow road leads to an inviting strand,
Covered with conch and kelp and mussel,
Where folks can sit and worship the sun,
Away from life's normal hustle and bustle.

The wind gnarled branches of the water oak,
Outline the life giving grassy marsh,
Showing the Makers artistic touch,
Painting landscapes with the elements so harsh.

The majestic Palmettos stand tall and straight,
Their sword like fronds bowing in adoration,
To our God who gave us the freedom,
From the tyranny by that past generation.

The lights and sounds from the jungle,
Create a veristic imitation of life,
With it's mysterious unknown quantity,
Of requited love and undesirable strife.

A spontaneous trip to Edisto Isle,
As to Solomon's palace of concubine,
Has it's pleasures beyond description,
At the discretions of yours and of mine.

Lovers with up raised arms and lips,
For kisses of the utter most adoration,
Inspired by the mystic Luna light,
And the surfs continuing palpitation.

Doctor Buzzard's secret magic potions,
Are not necessarily imbibed,
Just the scent of the boiling cauldron,
Makes the participants so inclined.

It's a compilation of our existence,
Teeming with life and smelling of death,
Still I'll be inundated with the island's romance,
'Till I breathe my very last breath!

The windblown palms bow like Moslems in a mosque!

The breaking waves glowed like sunlit crystal balls!

Still winter nights like loneliness in a deep dark cavern!

As Close As One's Own Breath

As I get older, sleep has become a real experience. Nightmares, epic dreams, talking and walking in my sleep seem to be the order of the night. In addition to that, my snoring, which didn't bother me, does disturb others in the house.

Praise the Lord, my wife, June, sleeps like a baby and is not bothered by the light when I turn it on to make notes for my next *Letters to the Editor*, poem, and anecdote of some of this curmudgeon's experiences or to read myself back to sleep. However, sleeping with me got more exciting when I started having those nightmares. One night, I decided that burglars were in our bedroom and that I had to defend my premises or more importantly my Guinevere. Full of the courage and the vigor, I had, twenty years ago, jumped out of bed and ran into the wall full speed knocking myself to the floor. I was OK with just a bit of blood.

Another night while wrestling a big black bear that had wandered into the bedroom, I rolled off the bed hitting my head on the *knobs* of the drawer on my bedside table. There was lots of blood that night.

While cleaning up my wounds the next day, my doctor sent me to a pulmonary specialist. Thankfully, my lungs were in pretty good shape but were just not getting quite enough oxygen as I slept (twenty-five years of heavy smoking, you know). She said that even a small amount of "oxygen deprivation" was like my brain reacting to a plastic bag being put over my head and with the panic attack that would create.

To solve that problem, they ordered an oxygen generator be brought to the home and set to the desired dosage with instructions as to its use. It was simple. Just turn it on and the small plastic tubing wrapped around my ears ending under my nose delivered the calming gas.

I cannot refrain from thinking about all of that as it relates to life in general and my religious life in particular.

We take in about 14,000 liters of air as we breathe some 26,000 times a day. That air is made up of 78 percent nitrogen, 21 percent oxygen, .94

percent argon, 0.04 percent carbon dioxide, some water vapor, and a few other trace gases. Of course, those proportions change, and not for the best, due to the amount of pollutants we ingest.

I see the world around us as a mixture of situations just as the air we inhale is a compound of gases. The improper proportion of life experiences is as deadly as would be the incorrect mixture of those vapors.

Perhaps the traditional seven deadly sins *pride, envy, gluttony, lust, anger, greed, and sloth* speak for themselves or would Mohandas Gandhi's interpretation *wealth without work, pleasure without conscience, science without humanity, knowledge without character, politics without principal, commerce without morality, and worship without sacrifice* be more applicable for our time. Living without a regard for those principals creates the lifestyle pollutants, which are as deadly to society as is the stuff we are pumping into the atmosphere is to our physical health.

Gandhi's "worship without sacrifice" covers the whole gambit of these listed sins. I believe that choosing *worship* in his list indicates his feelings that divine intervention is a (perhaps *the*) key to overcoming these sins.

God, recognizing the need for a roadmap for mankind to survive his trip on earth, gave Moses the Ten Commandments on Mount Sinai. As hard as mankind has tried to discredit them, those laws have held up for some thirty-five years. The opponents to living a spiritual law-abiding lifestyle are persuasive and strong. My only defense mechanism is a close relationship with the creator who gave us the "way, the truth, and the life."

In that regard, I think of a situation in *The Last Song,* a book in Jan Karan's Mitford series. Father Tim, who had been a pastor in Mitford for a number of years, is retired. He was called to be an interim pastor at a church in a small town down on the coast. The clannishness of the "to poor to paint and to proud to whitewash" aristocrats made the change to another ministry location very difficult for Father Tim.

Perhaps it was divine intervention that after he'd been on the job, just a few relatively ineffective months, a very destructive hurricane destroyed much of the town. Even most of the walls of their beloved church were not spared. But in that same church, the first Sunday after the storm, his message to his town of broken real estate and hearts, Father Tim preached his most spiritually healing sermon. The theme of that message was "no matter the circumstances, all is not lost as long as we keep God as close as one's own breath."

The Birds

Perhaps the most meaningful secular religious story I have heard is told every Christmas eve by *Paul Harvey*.

"Come on, Harry. I have the kids ready. The car is warming up, and it's time to go to the Christmas Eve service."

"If you don't mind, I think I'll just stay here in front of the fire and unwind. It's been a rough couple of weeks trying to get the year and numbers into the computer. Thanks for being so understanding and be careful. It's been snowing pretty good for the last few hours."

Harry was a good man, good husband, great father, honest workman, and generally a fine moral gentleman. Though he had trouble believing the *Chirstmas story,* he would, in no way, stand in the family's way of enjoying the "fable." Being a logical accountant that story was just not reasonable to him.

There is no point to a God becoming man. My gracious, in all of history, the opposite is true. Man and/or beings becoming or striving to become a god is the norm and if when they accomplished that the Gods established an elitist society using humans as some sort of slaves.

Why would an all-powerful God want to share one of his precious moments with the likes of man? And if he did, why would he choose to be born in an animal stall? No way! It's absurd!

Harry's thoughts were interrupted by something softly hitting his large picture window. Turning and looking out, he saw a flock of birds, attracted by the light in his window, flying into it and falling into the snow bank under the eves of the house. They were flopping dazed, confused, and apparently exhausted from their ordeal of being lost in the storm.

Moved by compassion, he went out, opened the garage door, turned on the light, and tried to shoo the birds into the warmth and safety of that building. But alas, the more he tried, the more they panicked. *Don't they know that I'm just trying to help them?* Then Harry thought, *If I could become like them, live with them, learn their ways, and could communicate with them—they would know what I am trying to do!*

Suddenly, a smile came over his face. The Christmas story was **no longer absurd.** He could picture that ordinary-looking infant, lying in that stable in Bethlehem, which provided the answer to his Christmas problem. God became one of us to offer us in human terms a way out of this chaos because he *loves us. God is love!*

Mary and the children came in a little after midnight, "Merry Christmas, Daddy."

"Merry Christmas, darling."

To this, Harry replied, "And may God continue to bless us . . . everyone!"

A Yule-tide Prayer

Dear God, thank you for putting into our hearts the ability to recognize the need for a time to, at the very least, acknowledge the angels' exaltation to the shepherds of "peace on earth, good will to a mankind."

Oh, sweet Jesus, our humble prayer continues and is for a happy winter festival, a Spiritually Rewarding Christmas, and/or Hanukkah and the wisdom to know the difference. Amen

Isn't it *strange* how our memories work? I just erased a portion of a story I wrote about a trip we took to Washington in the 1940s and how upset I was with my daddy when he would not let me go with him and Uncle Ed to see Babe Ruth and the Yankees play the Washington Senators.

It seems that Babe Ruth retired in 1937 after being traded to the Boston Braves. (He hit three home runs his last game.)

I cannot believe that thought is just a fantasy because it is so real. It certainly gives me some doubt as to my credibility as an historian.

Well, instead of a history, we'll call it a novel based on fact.

You may *question*—but please don't let that interfere with whatever enjoyment it may offer.

One of the most important things to remember about infant care is: never change diapers in midstream. Don Marquis.

I went to see Dr. Bowers concerning some blood pressure problems. "Well, my head was spinning pretty good yesterday while *blowing the driveway* clean."

And he said, "Did you ever think of using a leaf blower?" *Is that what those things are for?*

Because a noisy air conditioner was disturbing the services in our small Methodist Church; Dave, the chairman of the Trustees, got an estimate of the cost to repair and/or replace the damaged unit.

Since he could not attend the next board meeting, he had to depend on Pastor Watson to explain the problem to that body. Dave said, "Pastor, the *fan shaft* needs to be replaced. Now, do you understand it well enough so that you can explain it?

"Certainly I do," replied the preacher, "its biblical . . . like the shaft (chaff) which the wind driveth away. Psalms 1:4."

Preacher Don

Though I am a few years older than is Don, I knew him pretty well because our parents were good friends and church mates at the historic *Citadel Square Baptist Church* in downtown Charleston.

One fateful night while attending a revival conducted by Dr. R. G. Lee, a former pastor, I was a witness to Don's decision to dedicate his life to God through preaching his word!

The process of becoming a Baptist preacher involves being questioned by the *Board of Deacons* at an ordination hearing where if they, the spiritual leaders of the church, are "led" to accept your commitment, they will ordain you at the impressive *laying on of hands ceremony*. The chairman of that committee, my uncle Ward, told me that someone asked Don this question. "If we refuse to ordain you, what will you do?"; and for that, without hesitation, Don's reply was, "In all due respect, sin, as much as I covet your approval, I must remind you that it is God and not man who has called me to preach his Gospel, and preach it I shall . . . with or without this board's approval."

Don, who finished his formal education at the seminary and polished his pastoring techniques in some smaller congregations and was ultimately "called" as the youngest preacher ever hired to lead that Church where his spiritual life had been molded.

Though Don and I were not particularly close, since our lives had taken different directions, he was involved in one of the most memorable events of my life—a funeral over which he officiated profoundly influenced his (and as a matter of fact my) life.

As the final phase of that assemblage unfolded on a large sand hill, shaded by a giant oak tree, in Orangeburg County, Don concluded his eloquently delivered eulogy as he laid a perfect red rose on the polished bronze coffin that had been prepared to be lowered into that prehistoric ocean bottom. Accompanied by a late summer's evening breeze rustling the oak leaves, pine needles to a crescendo that equaled in beauty a Handel oratorio, he bid his spiritual mentor good-bye with this ancient Jewish blessing of God's love, hope, and peace. "Shalom, Brother Bill . . . shalom"!

Bill, a jolly, self-educated teacher, welder, bookkeeper, deacon, metal artist, hunter, fisherman, Grandfather, loving husband, brother and son was . . . *is. my daddy!*

A Letter I Wish That I Had Mailed to the Bishop and the Preacher!

While visiting several churches throughout the State, I have noticed that our denomination seems to be becoming long on ceremony and short on substance. To illustrate the point perhaps a freshman English comparative will help.

Excessive liturgy is to a healthy church as excessive cheese is to a healthy body.

In the beginning, it looks good and tastes good, but shortly, it begins to sap the "Living waters" of which the absence creates lethargy due to spiritual constipation. Eventually, the "arteries," that are essential for the growth of a healthy church body, become clogged with the cholesterol of complacency and boredom that limits the flow of that life-giving "blood of Jesus Christ." If not corrected, this leads to the disability and death of an otherwise healthy "body" which had the potential for a full service-oriented life. Some symptoms of that "artery disease" might be the demise of the ***Denomination Magazine,*** preachers not pastors, more concern with low golf handicaps than with high-quality visitations, pettiness at Board meeting, personal egos over Christian service, political correctness instead of spiritual correctness, and/or low Sunday school participation.

Too many of our preachers seem to be majoring in drama, creative writing, public relations, and sociology and too few in theology and pastoring.

To return to healthy Church bodies, we need to undergo the spiritual angioplasty that repairs the existing near useless arteries in the bypass surgery that replaces them. Either way, it will restore our vigor and allows the faith that features "Power in the Blood," "Washed in the Blood of the Lamb" and "Nothing But the Blood of Jesus" to re-nourish the "Body of Christ" that we laypeople allowed the leaders to neglect and make very ill.

Stroke Me?

I called the Methodist state offices looking for some direction in fund-raising for "WE CARE." After explaining my inquiry to the receptionist, she directed my call to another female. In the middle of my somewhat detailed request, she interrupted by saying, "Look, mister, I'm just a secretary." I accepted that, but recognizing the importance, I put on my clerical help when I was in business, I said, "And I'll bet you're a good one on whom your boss really depends." Though my reply was perhaps somewhat patronizing, it was intended to be sincere and kind. She apparently had some problem with it as her comment to me was, "Look, man, don't stroke me!"

I just hung up thinking, Woman's lib. versus Chivalry, perhaps that's what killed *King Arthur's Camelot* as it will destroy our beloved *Methodist Church!*

Sunshine Child

One Sunday, Pastor John Hipp brought tears as he told us the following story about how *love* creates miracles.

Johnny was four years old and an only child. It appeared that things would stay that way as the doctors told Mom and Dad that their chances of having another were next to none. But as so often happens through prayer, the impossible turned into a routine pregnancy. Ultrasound tests indicated that Johnny would soon have a little sister. He was so excited about the event that Mom would place his hand on her swollen stomach to feel the baby move. Johnny loved that little girl so much that he would press his nose right up to Mama's tummy and sing to her. Johnny only knew three songs: *Jesus loves me*; *happy birthday*; and his favorite song, which he sang to her at least once everyday.

The normal pregnancy ended with a delivery problem that kept the critically ill baby in intensive care for an extended period of time. Though either parent was constantly at the sick child's side, Johnny's pleading to see "his baby sister" was rejected due to hospital regulations. Finally, after more than a month of that, the parents relented, decided that he ought to be able to, at the very least, see "baby sister" just once before she dies.

Since it was a very cold evening, they were able to wear their overcoats to the hospital. When inside the building, the coats were used to wrap around Johnny to hide him until they could get to the infant intensive care unit. Though they got caught, much pleading with the attendant allowed Johnny "just a minute" with the small crib containing the tube-lanced child. He was not afraid but went directly to the transparent plastic crib and put his nose as close to his beloved baby sister as possible and began to sing, "You are my sunshine . . . my only sunshine . . . you make me happy when skies are gray . . . you'll never know, dear, how much I love you . . . *please don't take my sunshine away!*"

If you know where to look, almost any Sunday, you will find a proud six-year-old Johnny leading his two-year-old-sister Annie into her Sunday School Class.

Prayer takes many forms, doesn't it?

Yep, I Beat Her But . . .

Old Bethel Methodist Church near Simpsonville was dedicated around the year 1800 by a divinely inspired "circuit rider," Francis Asbury. The land for that church was donated by some of the great landowners in the area, and the money for building and maintaining the sanctuary was secured by using the capital earned from selling the cotton which had been raised on a piece of donated land (much like Erskine Caldwell's novel *God's Little Acre*).

The descendants of those "giving folks" still belong to **Bethel Church** and continue to live on the land that is left from the huge parcels that they sold to the "city slickers," Yankees, and golf course builders to fulfill the invaders' desire for country-club living.

One day, my friend Bill Taylor, who taught a lot of those folks in his Sunday School Class, told me about the Sunday old Mr. Earl Wilkins, wanting to make a point about how strict the Church used to be, spun this tale.

It seems that "Uncle Jessie" was called before the Church to decide if he should be "expelled" from the congregation for beating his wife. After the facts were presented to the membership, the pastor said to him, "Jessie, there is no question that you beat Aunt Bertha . . . now won't you at least say you're sorry?" After thinking for a few minutes, Jessie hitched up his trousers and stood as tall as his five-feet-four-inches would allow with a demeanor that would equal Stephen A. Douglas's as he debated "The Great Emancipator." Jessie said, "Ah jus can't ritely sa Ah'm sorry *ah* did it . . . but *ah* will say *ah'm* sorry ah had to!"

Thou Shalt Not Steal

Pastor Paul Frances was preaching his eighth sermon in a ten-part series on The Commandments. He began his message with his concern over "the pair who had recently robbed the Corn Grower's Bank just eight miles down the road in Delco." "Can you imagine their brazenness as they wore Richard and Pat Nixon masks while demanding an exact amount of money, 'no more, no less,' while repeating to anyone in hearing range, "I am not a crook . . . I am not a crook!" The pastor pulled himself up to his full five-feet-eight-inch height as he shouted his main point with emphatically, "To take something that is not rightfully yours is a sin against your fellowman and a sin against the God who made us and with whom we hope to spend eternity. If you continue to ignore God's laws, as sure as I'm standing in this pulpit, you're goin' straight to hell. Maybe you don't lie, take the Lord's name in vain, or chase your neighbor's wife around the house, but if you steal, yes, even if that's the only commandment you've broken . . . the Bible says—and I believe it—you might as well have broken them all, and you will be consumed by Satan's fires . . . *amen!*"

Though unusual, but not unprecedented in Methodism, Brother Frances had been pastor of Hope Methodist Church for seventeen years. They'd been good years spiritually in spite of the poor economic times in manufacturing-based small-town America. Prosperity, South Carolina, had not lived up to its name as the politicians did little to help its textile industry compete with those countries who allow, yea even encourage, slave labor wages. But in spite of the hard times, the church had survived with a pastor and a pastor's wife on whom they had come to depend and love. The preacher did not complain as they survived on a meager salary and the substance that the parishioners often brought. They were a loving and giving pastoral couple who were always ready to share what little they had with those in need. Yes, they even shared the old home place that they had inherited for the church to use as a parsonage.

He, his wife Bridget, God and, I suspect, even the family cat had began to believe that, after preaching almost fifty years, it was getting to be time to step aside and let the young folks take over. After all, Elder Rufus Lindler's boy, Luke, had just graduated from King's Bible College in Stateburg and needed a place to preach. Though the Elder would never say it outright, he surely did want Luke to preach here at Hope. Paul believed and had preached many times that "all things work together for good to them that love the Lord." And things were "working out." When he finished this go-round with the Ten Commandments, they had plans to serve the Lord in a different capacity.

Clancy, his wife Martha, and her brother, Otis, were regulars at church and usually sat on the right-hand side next to the last row of pews. Martha usually sat between them, but this Sunday, she stayed home—hot flashes, you know, and since the drugstore didn't open on Sunday, she had no way of getting the required dose of Lydia Pinkham's Vegetable Compound necessary to cool her down. "A lady just can't go to church and sweat like a longshoreman." Besides, if she stayed home, she could get some relief from the medicine (some called it shine) which Clancy made in a little machine (some call it a still) that he kept in the back of the barn. He used the product only for medicinal purposes, and since he seemed to be sick quite often, he took his "medicine" on a regular basis. In addition, it was supposed to protect folks from snakebite. Sure enough, since he started taking it regularly, he had not been bitten by a snake. Several doses a day seemed to keep him feeling pretty well most of the time. Martha didn't need the "shine" that often because she preferred Hadicol, which was recommended by her nondrinking Baptist friends. No matter that its main ingredient was alcohol. The fact that they bought this potent potable at the drugstore instead of the liquor store made it an acceptable Christian medication. But Clancy didn't mind her getting in his jug or taking the Baptist tonic. As a matter of fact, he encouraged her to maintain a two dose a day shine Hadicol regimen. It must be affective, since often after a "treatment," the two of them just sat in the porch swing and grinned at each other.

On their way home from church, Otis said to Clancy, "I can't believe that Martha missed church. She's always the one pushing us to go."

"Yep, you're right about that. She's a real churchgoer," replied Clancy.

"I remember one time we went over to Clydesburg to visit her cousin Gladys. Come Sunday and she wanted to go to church. The only place of worship nearby was something called The Christian Science Temple. She figured that all she needed was a Christian place to worship and that this sounded just fine. When she got home, I asked her how it was, and she said it was a little different but that it was OK." She continued, "I went in and sat down and after a time, this fellow got up and told what Mary Baker Eddy had done for him, then another fellow got up and said what Mary Baker Eddy had done for him. Next a woman in the front got up and told what Mary Baker Eddy had done for her. It went on and on like that 'till I could stand it no longer and stood up and told 'em what Lydia E. Pinkham had done for me."

Otis, choking on his cigar, said, "Oh, do now, Clancy . . . you know that didn't happen"!

Clancy replied, "You jus ask Martha if it didn't!"

Clancy continued the conversation with, "During the sermon this morning, I was wondering if somebody really and truly needed some money and stole it from someone who was rich and wouldn't miss it much or maybe even took it from a bank, do you think God would consider that stealing?"

"Gosh, Clancy, I just don't know. Maybe you ought to talk to the reverend about that."

Bridget Frances called to her husband, "Paul, it's Jeffery and Jannette Johnson. Can you get away from your study long enough to talk to them?"

"Y'all just come on in here. I've always got time for you. How's Leon doing since his fall? I know it's tough on a fourteen-year-old being out of commission so long!"

"Well, Pastor, it seems that crushed hand just won't heal, and he needs to have a bone transplant in order to be able to have a chance to use it again. The big thing is he's always been crazy about airplanes. Even now he's at the top grade permissible for one his age in the Civil Air Patrol program. That, plus being a straight "A" student, adds creditability to his dream of going to the Academy and becoming an air force officer. Things were looking real good for him until the accident. Now about his only chance to live this dream is to go up to Duke Hospital where they're doing the kind of bone transplants which could possibly help him. But that costs money . . . big bucks. I'm just about at my wit's end."

"Business is not good, and I'm mortgaged up to the hilt. Now I didn't come here to get money from you because I know that you're in the same shape as the rest of us. Since I was saved at your revival fifteen years ago and have tried to live the Christian life, I really believe in the power of prayer. Now I need a miracle! George Shemp told me that you and he prayed, and God kept the bank from foreclosing on his property."

At that, Pastor Paul, Bridget, and the Johnsons clasped hands, knelt around the coffee table, and prayed for God's will to be done.

The buzz around the barber shop was about the holdups of the Corn Bank about a month ago and at The Merchant's Bank of Holden yesterday. The crimes were similar, but this time, the thieves had on George and Barbara Bush masks. Barbara stood back as a lookout while George presented a note to the teller asking for a specific amount of money while saying, "Read my lips . . . no more . . . no less . . . read my lips."

Ralph wanted to know. "How much did they get?"

Josh chipped in, "We'll never know 'till they catch and try them. The bank just won't tell you! Preacher, you must be talking to the wrong folks or your message is falling on deaf ears."

Pastor just smiled and said, "The good book instructs me to sew the seeds as it warns me that some will fall on fertile ground while others will fall among the thorns and the stones."

There was much excitement up and down Main Street when they put up the wanted poster in the post office window offering a $5,000 reward for each of the bank robberies. It didn't show much as the facial features remained blank—the masks, you know. The descriptions were of two individuals, probably one male and one female, five feet ten inches, five feet six inches, 200 and 150 pounds, respectively, and of indeterminate age and race. They escaped in a 1939 black Mercury two-door vehicle.

"Don't sound like nothin' nobody round here would do. I'll bet it's some of those people from New Jersey who come down here to clear the land for that fancy new golf course. I told you that Country Club would bring trouble. They just ain't our kinda folks!"

The message this morning is about commandment number nine. Thou shalt not bear false witness! Liar liar pants on fire . . . nose as long as a telephone wire. I guess we're all glad that's not true or we'd be walking around alookin' mighty funny and in a lot of pain. Clancy, Martha, and Otis squirmed in their back-row seats as the sermon continued to its conclusion . . . "We promise over and over to do what God tells us is right, but being human, we fail. No matter though, if we're sorry, really sorry. God just keeps on forgiving and forgiving . . . It's called grace. Grace is love that we don't deserve, but he gives it anyway 'cause he loves us so much. Educated folks call it unmerited love. Sincerely ask his forgiveness right now, and he will give it willingly! Amen!"

The teller smiled as she said, "Bill and Hilary masks! Is this some kind of joke?"

"Lady just read the note and put up the money . . . no more . . . no less and nobody will be hurt. The truth is I never had sex with that woman."

The Hilary mask said over and over again, "What blue dress? . . . What blue dress?"

"Hello 911? . . . We've been robbed. This is the Cotton Picker's Bank in Eastside. They have on Bill and Hilary masks and just scratched off in an old black car. Hurry, you might catch them. No, I didn't see a gun, but I'm sure they had one."

Meanwhile someone called the parsonage, "Come quick, Pastor. Something awful has happened at the plywood mill." Just as they got there, EMS was hauling off a sheet-covered stretcher. Paul asked, "Who is it?"

"It's Bill Kimbull. The boiler blew up. He didn't have a chance!"

Pastor Paul asked, "Has anyone told Helen?"

"No, Pastor, we were waitin' for you."

Paul went by the parsonage and got Bridget, and they went over to the Kimbull home to give Helen the dreadful news that she is now a widow and that sixty-year-old Billy is now an orphan. "You know, Bridget, I never get used to this. Real old folks going to their rest is not so bad . . . even sometime cause for celebration, but to see a young family blown apart is just tough to handle."

A teary-eyed Helen forced a little smile as she said, "Without God's hand on my shoulder and your hand in mine, I could never handle it. Thank you for standing with me. I love you so much!"

After the funeral, Ed Simon asked, "Pastor, do you have time to talk to me for a few minutes sometimes tomorrow?"

"Sure, Ed, what about ten in the morning for coffee and maybe Bridget will have some of her homemade cinnamon rolls warmed up for us?"

"Sounds good. See you then."

When Ed arrived in a few minutes 'till ten, he didn't even have to knock because the pastor was on the porch in his rocking chair. "Pull up a chair, Ed, and if it's all right with you, we'll just talk out here. Excuse me a minute. Bridget, Ed is here."

"Thanks, Paul. I'll bring you some coffee and rolls in just a second"

"Thanks, sweetheart!"

As they enjoyed the morning treat, Ed began to talk, "We were so happy when Wanda married Jeff and though you did a beautiful job with the ceremony the knot just didn't get tied tight enough. He just can't stay away from the gambling, booze, and other women. She has taken him back over and over again but is finally at the end of her rope. He won't work but has managed to charge all of their credit cards up to the limit. Since the mill has closed, I'm living off my savings . . . I just cannot help her. She's got a decent job and just needs for the creditors to give her time to pay them off. Padre. please pray with me that she will be able to work her way out of this situation. And oh yes, one more thing, she's gonna have a baby. Her husband raped her when she kicked him out." And the preacher and the concerned father knelt right there on the porch and prayed, "Please help us but, of course, Thy will be done!"

Cory rushed into the barber shop shouting, "I just heard it on my scanner. They've done it again. John and Jackie Kennedy just robbed the bank over at Jones' Corner. Well, maybe it wasn't them, but whoever did it, had on the masks, and he kept saying, 'Ask not what your bank can do for you rather ask what you can do for your bank. Just read the note and put the money I asked for in the bag ... no more ... no less. What am I gonna do for your bank? I'm making it famous!'" Then they drove away in a very fast old black car.

"This Sunday concludes our series on the Ten Commandments, and it's appropriate that it also concludes our ministry in this church. We shall not cry because it's over because we are so blessed that it happened. God is allowing us to continue our ministry at a mission school in Nigeria on the continent of Africa."

The message of the Tenth Commandment, thou shalt not covet, went as planned but was in most cases blocked out by the preacher's and the congregation's memories of seventeen wonderful and blessed years. "I said at the beginning that we shall not cry and we will do our best to live up to that boast but perhaps being compassionate Christians, you will allow us a private tear or two. We'll be back soon because the mission board has only allowed us to commit for only two years." Then with a slight break in his voice, Pastor said, "In the late 1950s Nat King Cole had a hit song which included lyrics that the Lord led me to accept as a way of life. It goes like this ... 'The greatest thing you'll ever learn is just to love and be loved in return.' You lived that message with us. We love you and always shall! Thank you and may God continue to bless you every one!"

Epilogue

Mr. Billy Kimbull
Prosperity, South Carolina.

Dear Billy,

Ms. Bridget and I are settling down with our work at the Christian School here in the jungles of Nigeria. We know that since losing your dad, things have been pretty tough for you and your mom, but you must not worry. God will provide. Now, in that regard, it's important that you follow the instructions in this letter very closely and quickly.

Go to the post office and get a copy of the poster offering the $5,000 reward for catching the robbers of each of those five banks. Take that and this letter to Sheriff Frick and go with him to our home, "the Parsonage," and look in the back of the barn where you will find a movable false wall behind the pile of hay bales. Behind that wall, you will find a 1939 black Mercury automobile, an assortment of rubber masks, which resemble the faces of several presidents, some shoes with two-inch lifts, and some padded clothing. In addition, you will find five bank bags, each containing $3,000. Take the bags and the money back to the banks whose names are on the bags.

The reward should amount to $25,000. Take $5,000 of that money and give it to Ed Simon's daughter, Wanda, and the other $20,000 is for your mama and for your operation at Duke Hospital.

Nigeria does not have an extradition treaty with the United States, so we will not be available to the sheriff until we return home in two years ... just in time for you to begin college. We love you, and may God bless you all!

Love,
Pastor and Mrs. Paul Frances.

Inspired by an idea of my beloved wife, June Bowen.

Forgive Us Our Trespasses

Prologue

Being paroled after only two years of their five-year sentences was the answer to many prayers. Though most all were surprised, no one expected less than good behavior from Pastor Paul and Bridget Frances. I suspect that the judge took that into consideration as the law extracted its "pound (or perhaps half a pound) of flesh" from those modern-day Robin Hoods.

Since Prosperity, South Carolina, was one of the many victims of our government's failure to protect small-town America and its textile industry from the unfair third world slave wage competition, money for even the basic necessities was in short supply. Thus, Pastor Paul decided, even at the risk of his and Bridget's freedom, to find a way to fill some of those needs.

As they tried to make right any wrongs they had done, while they were on their missionary journey to Nigeria, they confessed their crimes by giving Billy Kimbull the evidence he needed to turn them in and collect the $25,000 reward. The money was to be put to good use to correct a medical problem which kept him out of the Air Force Academy and to help Wanda Simon, who was pregnant due to being raped by her ex-husband. Despite the fact that the stolen money had been returned, and the reward money was put to good use, society had to be paid its due.

The Story

Since the "powers that be" in the Methodist hierarchy were deliberating the disposition of the pension of this ex-con priest, Pastor Paul had no income. His almost sixty years of faithful service conflicted with the condemnation by The Discipline (the Methodist book of laws) concerning clergy who committed crimes. Their quandary was, were there extenuating circumstances? But then let's proceed with the original tale because that's a story for another time.

The Lindler family had been leaders at First Church for more than six generations. The office of Elder had seemingly been passed down from grandfather to father to son but none ever went into the ministry. That is none until Elder Rufus Linder's son, Luke, was called to preach. Conveniently he graduated from the seminary about the time of Pastor Paul's retirement. So Luke would be the logical successor to Paul as Pastor of The First and Only Methodist Church of Prosperity. The board voted to call him and, with the Bishop's approval, he became Pastor Luke.

Pastor Paul had been the guiding hand that led Luke through his sometimes-turbulent teen years and into young adulthood with a minimum of the usual scars often accrued in the battle of hormone-induced adolescence. Now the tide had turned. The teacher was in need of spiritual and emotional guidance from the student.

Without any guaranteed income, the Franceses had no choice but to return to their home in Prosperity. That, of course, added to the trauma of being released from prison and the anticipation of how the home folks would accept ex-cons as their neighbors.

Clancy and Martha Metz were the first to welcome Paul and Bridget home as they picked the pastor up at the railroad station. The thirty-mile trip home was filled with trepidation and a quest for information about the folks and the town itself. The report was that the people were existing with neighbor helping neighbor. The town was not faring so well as businesses were closing and the buildings were becoming dilapidated due to a lack of maintenance. The church, under the rapidly maturing leadership of Pastor Luke, remained the glue which held whatever was left together.

As they drove through town, the streets seemed almost deserted. Perhaps things were even worse than they had heard. But then, as they got closer to the old home place, the traffic seemed to be picking up. Suddenly they noticed that cars were parked everywhere, and folks were standing along the sides of the road waving and cheering. The house had a new paint job à la Martha's brother Otis, the lawn had been cut, and the flower beds weeded by Bill Kinbull and his newly repaired hand, and inside was spick and span due to the efforts of the Woman's Society led by Wanda Simons and Helen Kimbull. The tables were full of enough food to feed the crowd. Plus the cupboard and frig were overflowing due to the "pounding" participated in by everybody in the town. If indeed, "home is where the heart is" there is no question that these ex-cons were welcomed back home.

After a few days of getting settled down physically and emotionally, they were ready to receive visitors. One of the first was young Pastor Luke. "Come in here, Luke, and sit down for a cup of tea. To what do we owe this honor?"

"Well, Pastor Paul, this is more than just a social visit."

Without a lot of formalities, Luke got right to the point. "This town and this church need ya'll's help. As a result of the loss of jobs, the money needed to sustain any kind of lifestyle is running out. Without a solution in sight for the foreseeable future, the normal upbeat nature of these folks is starting to run mighty thin. I just don't know how long these proud folks can continue as more and more of them are having to depend on those despicable government handouts. We know the church's 'high monkedy monks' are still making up their minds about your pension and that until they decide on your status as a Methodist minister, you cannot serve in any official capacity and that your money is in short supply. So we at First Church want to offer you a job as the church custodian by using some of the mission money we would normally send to the conference. You wouldn't have to do any cleaning as we already do that ourselves. We just need your wisdom and council. 'Sounds like mission work to me.'"

The pastor was overwhelmed and commented, "We have a roof over our heads, thanks to ya'll enough food to last for a long time and can pay the electric bill with what little savings we have, so give 'unto God what is God's,' and we'll be here if you need us. Let's you and I pray. 'Father, we praise you, we love you and thank you for all that you do for us. Now once again we need your help. You know our problems. We just ask that thy will be done and that you might help us help ourselves, amen!'"

The pastors decided that if the town was to help itself, the best place to start would be for a group of some influential citizens to meet at the mayor's office. They agreed on a time and sat down to discuss the situation. There were several ideas, some as trite as having scheduled flea markets, bake sales, and/or a Cotton Pickin' Festival with street dances, parades, and all. During the discussion, Jeff Cory added that while hunting rabbits over by the deserted mill, he had run into Mr. George Coleman, the owner. Mr. George had always been a generous employer and showed his concern for all of "his people." He mentioned to me that his legal staff had come up with a suggestion which could be mutually beneficial. With all of the textile plant closings, the buildings which housed them are not worth a dime a dozen. So their only chance for any return on that investment would be to create a tax write off situation by donating the property to a nonprofit organization. We could qualify for that gift if we would set up a charitable trust with definite goals for any money gained through the use of those buildings.

At that Mayor Derrick spoke up and suggested that he call a town council meeting to discuss this proposition. He added, "In the meantime, please be thinking about this . . . all that glitters is not gold. We would acquire certain liabilities such as upkeep and insurance to protect against any accidents which might occur on the property. Are we in a position to take that chance?"

At that, the group retired to the coffee shop and settled down for small talk and their cups of coffee and sweet rolls. Just as they were served, Otis came running in all out of breath, "Help me . . . help me! . . . I might die! Git me to the clinic as soon as possible!"

Pastor Paul spoke up, "What in the world is wrong with you, Otis?"

"Well, last night, my hemorrhoids started itching so bad that I got up in the dark and went in the bathroom to find my Preparation H. I forgot my glasses but found a tube anyway and used a whole bunch of it. I gasped, waking up Marcie, as I realized that something was just not right. Marcie came running in and yelled, 'What are you doing with my Polygrip and look you've smeared that dental adhesive all over your butt!'"

At that, Otis screamed again, "Get me to the doctor in a hurry. I done glued my behind together."

At the called council meeting, while discussing the pros and cons of taking on a project of such magnitude, Ed Simon, who owned the saw mill, spoke up, "I got an idea. This guy was in the other day and left me his calling card and said for me to call him if I knew of anybody who had a grove of hardwood for sale. It seems that those Yankees are using all they can get on their fancy floors and furniture. While he was talking, I remembered when they built those mills they had to have very strong floors to hold up those heavy looms and spinners. We just might be able to use that thick oak and hickory if we would re-mill it into boards suitable for home and business use. I know there's a market there and that we could get a pretty penny for it from those New York folks."

The mayor thought that was a good beginning but that they needed more than a short-term solution. At that, Jeff Cory, a real estate broker, spoke up, "If Ed had not jumped in first, he was going to give them his idea. As you know, this area is close to the lake, has good schools, and parts of our county is growing like crazy. I was reading the other day that the trend in housing is going toward apartment and condo living. These young homeowners just don't want to be tied down with yard and home upkeep. They work hard and long and want any spare time they have to go to personal and family recreation time. The folks in Columbia are doing a bang-up job selling, at a premium price, space in the old department stores and mills to perspective homeowners—"

Pastor Luke broke in, "We could replace the hardwood floors with pine and use some of the money from the sale of the hardwood to build the living areas. With our initial investment and tax base being pretty low, we could offer those folks some bargain priced good ole country living away from the hustle and bustle of downtown."

Pastor Paul added, "Plus this would give some jobs to our citizens and allow us some money for the improvements and maintenance to keep our town a good place to live. Further . . . the stores downtown would benefit from the extra business." He bowed his head, closed his eyes, and prayed, "Thank you, dear God, for your mercies!"

With the addition of a playground, a swimming pool, a walking track, and a putting green, the development of The Prosperity Arms took off like a rocket. As expected, jobs caring for the property, and those generated by sales in the business area, allowed the little town of Prosperity, South Carolina, to once again live up to its good name.

Meanwhile, the First and Only Methodist Church with Pastor Luke "increased in wisdom and in statue and in favor of God and man!"

Epilogue

And guest Pastor Paul stood tall in the pulpit of The First and Only Methodist Church of Prosperity. His sermon topic was Forgive Us Our Trespasses. "Yes, forgive us our trespasses as we forgive those who trespass against us. Our God is the loving and forgiving God who wants us to spend eternity with him. But as much as he wants to forgive us, he will not without our true desire to be with him on his terms. We must accept him as our savior, beg forgiveness, try to sin no more, and forgive our fellowman. Do we really believe as we pray, 'Forgive us our trespasses as we forgive those who trespass against us. It all ties together as we believe on the Lord Jesus Christ and are saved. Amen!'"

We will now receive your gifts to God!

At that, there was an audible gasp from the congregation as the ushers were all wearing Richard Nixon masks and repeating, "Do not be a crook. Put into the plate what you believe God is due. No more . . . no less!"

A Tribute to My Friend

Conrad Graham was a natural born salesman. I ought to know since we were business competitors for a long time, as a matter of fact, sometimes much too long.

He had the innate ability to make people smile. His God created in him that talent, in the words of the late great Nat King Cole, "To love and be loved in return."

That love was limitless, and he was always ready to share it among his large family. I challenge you accept and to live with that gift of adoration which Papa Rod provided for each and every one of us!

I have to smile through the tears because, though he's gone, we were so blessed to have him as long as we did.

His testimony shall be missed in the Jolly Christians, Friends, The Christian Fellowship Sunday School Class, Thursday morning Bible study, men's club, The Misfits Kitchen Band, and those who are handicapped to whom he attended, he touched many lives. If you don't believe it, you should have tried when you were with him, to get out of the grocery store, Hardees or anywhere else without him talking to the people there.

As a personal thing, my June and I shall experience a real void without Rod on our future trips and voyages. But I know he'll be there in spirit for a long, long time.

We have an empty spot in our hearts, yes, we're gonna miss him in all the old familiar places. But in my mind's eye, I shall always see him in front of the Misfits with his instrument, a cheese grater, and a spoon, closing our performances with this bit of wisdom.

That First *Real* Kiss

The old song that said "Oh, that kiss in the dark was to you just a kiss but to me was a thrill divine" describes fully my feeling in that seventh grade school year on a September eve at Pansey Huckabee's party.

My experience with kissing prior to that evening was limited to the slight pecks on the cheek of my female parent, aunts, and grandmothers. I never knew what I had been missing!

"And now the rest of the story!"

I felt really dressed up in my best khaki pants (starched so stiffly that I could hardly bend my knees), sport shirt buttoned at the collar (stiffly starched), and freshly scrubbed sneakers on my feet. My hair was squeaky-clean and held in place with the *Rose Oil hair Tonic*, which I had just bought for 10¢ from Kress' Dime Store. There was not a Citadel plebe that stood straighter, prouder, or smelled as sweet as did I on that night when I stopped by to pick up my buddy Walter Tylee for the five-block walk to the destination of our first trip into emotional Utopia.

We lived at Carter's Place (we called it Carter's Alley) which was located off Heriot Street across from the V. C. Fertilizer plant. The Huckabees lived in a very nice area (with lawns) at the end of Mt. Pleasant Street on the Ashley River. Though the atmosphere seemed miles apart, the actual distance was just a short walk from the moonlike terrain of "the alley" to that neighborhood which resembled the landscaping of Middleton Gardens. We had no grass because the fertilizer was so thick that the only plants which could survive the foul air were the *canna lilies* that grew higher than my daddy's head.

Walter and I used the time it took for the walk to the party to "spruce up" a bit by brushing that ever-present fertilizer from our respective shoulders. Just as we arrived Pansey said, "Everybody sit down here . . . boy-girl . . . boy-girl, etc." She then produced a Coca Cola bottle which was laid on its side before she spun it. When the bottle stopped spinning, it was pointing at Jeff Owens, who grabbed Pansey and kissed her right on the lips while everybody watched and giggled. Then it was Jean Ott's time to spin, and the

167

same thing happened when it pointed at Billy Mott. I reached behind Marilyn Clarke and tapped Walter. As he looked into my eyes, I could see the fear that, to the best of my knowledge, had only been there once before, at the scariest monster movie we ever attended. Though I did my best to be "cool," if the fearful eyes didn't give me away, I'm sure, the giant drops of sweat sliding off my nose did.

The near panic attack was interrupted by Marilyn saying excitedly, "Billy, it's pointing at you! *Kiss me!*" All twelve years of my life flashed before my eyes, thank goodness for the drain near by, which kept my sweat puddle from overflowing into my sneakers.

Before I could escape, she grabbed me with a pucker as large as an 8 oz. funnel. But alas, somehow we missed, and I got my lip caught in the poodle-shaped stickpin in her scarf. Luckily, I am a quick healer and didn't bleed much and luckily (again), the massive sweating obscured the tears that are normal from a pinprick on the lips. I had no place to go, so I bravely endured the ridiculing laughter of my peers. The game continued!

Then it happened! Patricia Rhodes, that vision of pure loveliness with Liz Taylor's ebony hair and violet eyes, spun the bottle, and it pointed at me. Her beauty created a reflex action that forced me to gently, though somewhat clumsily, kiss her right on the lips. Not even the primitive anesthetics, that I had experienced with my several ear operations, made my head spin as did that *first real kiss.*

As the evening wore on, our trepidation concerning the kissing games turned into a desire to participate more fully. At the request by the hostess for couples to indulge in a game of *Five Minute Dates*, with a wink, Walter grabbed Marilyn and took off for the rose arbor, while Patricia and I slipped away to the boat dock. As we strolled to our respective "date spots," we could hear the rhythmic chanting of our friends singing, "Don't make love by the garden gate. Love is blind but the neighbors ain't!"

PS. Patricia's family moved across the Ashley River and St. Andrews School for the seventh grade through high school. She was "Homecoming Queen and Miss St. Andrews High School. We never dated but were buddies."

Lymricks

With three girls, seven grands, and a cat,
Half a century has gone. Just like that.
You know it's been fun,
It's been a great run,
And we cherish the love we begat!
St. Patrick set Ireland free,
With shamrocks for the snakes he made flee.
It's the emerald Isle,
Why not go there a while.
With Colleens, Jigs, whisky and Tralee!
It's been six months since September 11,
The world's in distress, the continents all seven.
Though the universe wants peace,
and for the terror to cease,
All's well 'cause God's in his heaven!
They call Erin the Emerald isles,
But Edisto's a diamond, all the miles.
The breeze blows the palms,
and our stress into calms,
and turns our frowns into smiles.
There was once a young lady named June,
Whom I wooed by Fort Moultrie's sand dune.
Though we've laughed and shed tears,
For some fifty-eight years,
When she gives me the eye, I still swoon!
Do you remember that lady named June,
Whom I wooed by that Low Country moon?
Though five decades have gone,
She still turns me on.
We old folks still know how to spoon.

Mitzi

In 1945, while in the seventh grade, the light of my life was the beautiful Mitzi, who returned that feeling of affection at least *until* the junior-senior dance. (We had grammar school graduation ceremonies, baccalaureate services, and a junior—senior dance just as they did in high school). I had clearly expanded my social circle as we lived in a modest five-room wooden bungalow while her family lived in a two-story brickhouse "with more than one bathroom." They were obviously well-off and quite able to offer a much better than average lifestyle for their little debutante. But in spite of the economic differences, I was accepted by her family, due a great deal, to the fact that I decided to make payoff the agony Mama inflicted on me while using "the ruler across the knuckles method" of teaching "manners."

On the night of that fateful dance, I thought that I looked pretty good in spite of the fact that the hand-me-down blue suit was somewhat threadbare. But we, the suit and I, were so clean and shiny that we were able to project an aura that hid many of the fabric's shortcomings.

As the door of her home opened in answer to the chimes I shall never forget that vision of loveliness draped in crinolines covered by a blue strapless gown. The dress was beautiful and fit her perfectly in spite of the fact that it was obviously held up by something like scotch tape in order to ensure the modesty of one whose cleavage would barely be discernible in a wet T-shirt.

The guys decided that we would give our dates either orchid or carnation corsages and all did . . . that is all did except me . . . when, ever frugal and domineering, Grandma convinced Daddy, who had inherited at least the first of those traits, that it was a waste of money to pay a florist for such a simple task.

So there I stood in the doorway of the home of the most beautiful creature on earth, in full view of her parents, grandparents, aunts, uncles, and assorted cousins who had gathered to celebrate her entrance into the world of dating. Yes, there I stood in a shiny blue suit bearing a sweet pea corsage the size of something they put over the shoulder of the winner of the Derby.

As *puberty* increased its intensity in the age-old battle against **Childhood** for our psyche, our search for an information source increased in intensity. Since our literary sources only created "an itch," we desperately needed something or somebody to instruct us in the art of "scratching."

Buddy's elder brother Sonny, a high school junior, seemed perfectly willing to, yea, even anxious to, accommodate us by becoming the sexual mentor of we three noncompetitive disciples. Few groups have ever been more willing learners. We became Plato to Sonny's Socrates and Aristotle to his Plato as our discussions rivaled the "dialogues" that led to the creation of the **Republic** and the **Timaeus**. Just as the great philosophers had instructed their pupils on the principals of solving the universal problems of justice, the nature of government, and the workings of the universe, Sonny used his vast reservoir of knowledge, gained from his myriad conquests, to counsel us in the fine art of utilizing our newly found human sexuality.

So the back steps of 126 Live Oak Avenue became our Athenaeum.

Tales concerning drive in theaters, a shiny red convertible, fogged car windows, campfires, tubs of beer in the dunes, and constant phone calls from every female classmate were the texts from which our credits in sex ed 101 were earned.

The lectures continued until one day a car full of the very same girls who had been calling Sonny rode by with Hank, the "school Romeo," behind the wheel. Lola, the "hottest thing in school" was by his side. As they passed, Hank yelled, "Hey, Sonny Boy, don't you ever run with the big guys?"

And as they drove away, the others, led by Lola, taunted, "Sonny boy is a virgin! *Sonny* is a *virgin! A virgin! A virgin!*"

Of course, Sonny's image had been so tarnished, in the eyes of those *thirteen-year-olds*, that the "dialogs" had to be abandoned, and we were again left to our own devices in our quest for the "forbidden knowledge."

Though the foregoing paragraphs of this anecdote were lighthearted, this *absolutely true* conclusion will not be as flippant.

Lola was a Senior—the Homecoming Queen, the prettiest girl in school, and an "A" student. Hank was a junior—a star football player, a class officer, and a pretty good student.

Lola got pregnant and had to drop out of school three months before graduation!

Hank married Lola. The families supported them in allowing Hank to continue his education at a private school (no marrieds allowed in public school) and by supplementing the salary he earned as a grocery clerk enough to give them a reasonable—no frills lifestyle.

Gone were Lola's honors, graduation, and college. Gone were Hank's football scholarship, graduation with his friends, and the marriage! They were divorced in less than a year, and the child care payments began!

Buddy, his brother, and the rest of their family moved to Charlotte, so I never got to tell Sonny.

Sonny boy is a real man! Sonny is a real man! Real man! A man!

Family Kissin'

My family has never been real big on kissing. Just a quick buzz or peck on the cheek seemed to work very well on both sides—the Shinglers and the Bowens.

Now, what Grandma Bowen lost in her desire to create a kissing dynasty was made up for in her ability as a first-class hugger. She went at it with such enthusiasm that you had to be very careful not to get your nose caught in her ample bosom for fear of suffocation. In that regard, I am told of a meeting between her and some of the senior family members, where they demanded that she limit her hugs to one minute or less after we found that at least one uncle and three cousins contracted brain damage due to oxygen deprivation.

In ours, as in most families, there are exceptions to the rule. We had Aunt Marion, who was married to Grandmama Shingler's brother Eugene (Uncle Gene) from Massachusetts. He was the last of the descendants of my great-great-great-grandfather, the famous (some think infamous) General Artimus Ward (by the way, that is true) I'm not sure of the facts of his combat experience, but it is whispered that while looking for "Red Coats" at the resorts in Cape Cod, he had two horses and three Red Cross nurses shot out from under him (bad! I borrowed it from L. Grizzard), but I digress back to my story.

Aunt Marion and her daughter, Frances, about five years older than I, were the kissin'est people I ever seen. You could be just walking down the hall, and they would grab you and kiss you right on the lips for no apparent reason except that you were just handy. Daddy and I didn't hang around the house much when they were there. However, one purpose was apparently served since my "pucker power" has (modestly reported) never been complained about.

Oh yes, one last thing, Frances later married some guy named Roger, a tall skinny fellow with *real big feet*.

I understand that they had a house full of kids (huummm).

Puppy Love

Back in my day, first love between adolescent couples was *puppy love*. It was often a situation, as is usual in most early romances (or, heck, like most all romances), where the girl leads the poor guy around by his nose, and he is so "goo goo eyed" over her he doesn't realize it. How that specific female person can suddenly appear out of nowhere and change a bright, active, twelve-year-old male athlete, for whom a black eye and skinned knee gained proving his athletic prowess is a badge of honor, into a slithering mass of raging hormones wimp ... when she "gives him the eye" ... is a mystery known only by those of that gender.

In that regard, because of the encouragement of my twin football playing uncles, whom I had always admired as big brothers, I went out as a freshman for the high school team during spring practice. With much hustle and enthusiasm, I did surprisingly well. So with the voids on the team created by graduation, a few added pounds of muscles, my dream of George, Lewis, and Billy, starting together on the same squad, became a distinct possibility. With that in mind, I spent most of the summer working with my carpenter Granddaddy, running, and eating to gain the necessary weight, stamina, and muscle to compete for a position. My body responded favorably, and things were looking very good until ...

Well, the cliché about the "best laid plans of mice and men ..." happened to me again, when the lovely Mary Anne moved right next door about three weeks before the start of football practice. It took only a few days until I became the best example of the aforementioned effects of "puppy love" imaginable.

I just barely made the team, but certainly not the starting team! Upon realizing this, I said to my Mama, "I don't know what happened. I had it made, but then I blew it. I'm not hungry ... have no energy ... I can't even concentrate enough to learn the plays! What's wrong with me, Mom, am I sick?"

To that, she replied, "Billy, I really don't think you can call it a sickness, but I do know ... *that* ...

"Puppy love leads to a dog's life!"

Patriotism

Gone but Not Forgotten

The love of God, family, and country is manifest through celebrations such as Christmas, Yom Kipper, family members' birthdays, and national events of significance.

A time for such celebration is close at hand with Memorial Day and the birthday of one of our greatest presidents in May and early June, respectively.

He was born in 1808 in Christian (now Todd) County Kentucky, the tenth child of Samuel and Jane. Joseph, his oldest brother, moved to Natchez to practice law and raise cotton where he amassed a fortune and used it to lift his family from obscurity. The family then migrated to Louisiana. At age seven, he took a thousand-mile journey back to Kentucky on horseback with family friends to attend a Catholic seminary. At nine years of age, he attended Jefferson Academy in Mississippi; at thirteen, he returned to Kentucky to attend Transylvania University; and at sixteen, entered West Point where he graduated.

He fought in the Black Hawk War under Colonel Zackary Taylor, later married Taylor's daughter and moved to Mississippi where Sarah, his wife, died from malaria fever after only three months of marriage. From 1835 to 1845, he was a planter in seclusion building a successful plantation until he finally overcame his grief, and in 1845, he was elected to Congress and married Varina Howell.

When war came with Mexico, he organized the Mississippi Rifles and fought under the command of his old father-in-law, General Zackory Taylor. He won praise from General Taylor for his gallantry and national praise for his creation of and implementation of the V-formation attack that saved General Taylor's forces from almost certain disaster.

Wounded and still on crutches, he returned home and was elected Senator from Mississippi. In 1853, he was appointed Secretary of War where he enlarged the army, revised its tactics, and made improvements at West Point.

In 1862, he was inaugurated as president.

After his presidency, his opponents shackled him and put him in jail for two years, after which he was released on $100,000 bail and, though he pleaded for years to be brought to trial, he never was given that "inalienable right." His fortune wrecked, his home ruined, and his health impaired; he lived many of his last years in poverty except for the charity of his admirers. In 1884, at the insistence of the governor and the legislators, the feeble but firm seventy-six-year-old addressed the state legislature and stated, "If I were to do it all over again, I would do just as I did in sixty-one."

He died on December 6, 1889, and was buried with the adoration of more people, from every walk of life, than had ever attended a funeral in the South. This couldn't happen! The historians of the day said that he was a hated man. We all should be so hated!

In his last speech, which was to a group of young people, he said, "The past is dead, let it bury its dead, its hopes, and its aspirations; before you lies the future—a future full of expanding national glory, before which all the world shall stand amazed. Let me beseech you to lay aside all rancor, all bitter sectional feeling, and to make your places in the ranks of those who will bring about a consummation devoutly to be wished—a reunited country."

The New York Herald in an editorial said, "In the essential element of statesmanship, he will be judged as the rival and parallel of Lincoln. When the two men came face-to-face as leaders of two mighty forces, bitter was Northern sorrow that Providence had given the South so ripe and rare a leader and the North an uncouth advocate from the woods."

The New York World said, "A great soul has passed away."

The London Herald observed, "Successful or fallen, tried on untried, condemned or uncondemned, he is to us the greatest man in America.

Since his life was saved from the assassin's bullet, his reputation had to stand up to the biased reporting of those who never shy away from historical revisionism. Serious students of history (the vast minority of the self-styled intellectualist) have separated those whose reputations are enhanced by the great filter of martyrdom that leaves only which some wish to be considered and makes gods and demigods out of the demagogues and demireps and those who live a full life of honor.

Jefferson Davis, under any measurement of character and ability, is on a par with any and is head and shoulders above the rest.

So on May 10, Confederate Memorial Day, and on June 3, Jefferson Davis's Birthday, when you see my flags, the Stars and Stripes and the Stars and Bars (with the seven stars on the blue field and the three stripes of red and white) flying side by side, I'll join you, from the North, in a chorus of "Battle Hymn of the Republic" if you will join me in a verse of "Dixie."

Then let's shake hands, raise our eyes to heaven and our voices to a higher level and prayerfully sing the most meaningful song of all, "God Bless America."

The Supplication

World War II was an exciting time for this twelve-year-old. The very effective propaganda machine did its job of keeping our morals high by convincing us of our invincibility. The "cause" was glamorized as H. V. Kaltenborn gave the highly censored news on radio, and John Wayne et al., outsmarted the stupid but cruel enemy at every turn in the movies.

We bought war bonds and stamps, saved tin foil, metal cans and grease, tolerated rationing, shortages, and overcrowding, had defense rallies, and learned to spray and not shoot a direct stream of water at an incendiary bomb. Endured blackouts, and shout of the air raid warden when light shone through our heavy curtains and auto headlights painted black halfway down to keep the light from attracting German U-Boats.

The first stages of growing up began as the realities of war started to overcome the heroic fantasies presented by the media. Even a serendipitous preteen, such as I, could feel the pain of friends and relatives as the blue pendants with the white stars that hung in the windows to signify a son, daughter, or husband in service, turn to gold to signify killed in action. I remember trying to suppress a tear while asking Mama, "You mean no more rides on John Signeous's motor cycle . . . you mean my buddy is not coming back . . . you mean he's dead . . . ?"

I shall never forget that September night in 1943 when the personal aspect of the war really hit me. As Mama and I were leaving the Gloria Theatre (Daddy worked night shift at the Navy Yard), after having seen the movie Casablanca, there was excitement in the streets. The crowds were milling around, a few of the neon lights that had been turned off until the "duration" were on, and the newspaper boys were hawking their papers by shouting, "Extra . . . extra . . . Read all about it . . . Italy surrenders to the allies!"

The shouting, dancing in the streets, hugging and kissing and cries of joy that were the forerunner of other such celebrations that would equal or surpass this first of a series of victories was muted by something taking place right next to me.

184

There stood a mother hugging her sandy-haired two-year-old daughter crying her heart out, mixing adult's tears of trepidation with child's tears of wonder, sobbing her phrase of hope, "he's comin' home . . . he's comin' home . . . Your Daddy's *coming home to United States!*" At that point, my adolescent cries of, "We beat the lard out of those greasy Italians" became a more mature prayer of "please, God, don't let war ever happen again."

Though we have since fought in Korea, Vietnam, Granada, Desert Storm, and others, that prayer is as fervent as ever, but it has, I believe, become a wiser, more mature supplication of "please, God . . . peace with honor!"

Hang in There

To a talented friend who can't seem to break into the system and is distressed over the corporate rejections:

Most people are neither talented nor creative enough to do enough to get rejected. Rejections are OK though hard to accept. Show me a good loser, and I'll show you a constant loser. (I really believe I made that up. Not bad, I'll say) Of course, acceptance is better. I'll have to admit, but when you are rejected, at least you know that you have given yourself a chance to win!

To keep from getting discouraged and despondent, we must set goals (most of which are attainable).

        Goal 1: To Create
        Goal 2: Self-acceptance
        Goal 3: Some Peer Acceptance
        Goal 4: Acceptance by "The World"

Recognize the fact that most of "The World," for whatever reason, cannot or will not establish nor attain any goals.

From Gray's Elegy in a Country Churchyard . . .

Full many a gem of purest ray serene
The dark unfathomed depths of ocean bear
Full many a flower is born to blush unseen
And waste its sweetness on the desert air.

Would the world have been better off without those flowers or gems? I think not! Wherever beauty—written or otherwise—is created, something, someone, or even just the creator is better off.

One of the best uses of originality is to say common things in an uncommon way.

He who thinks for himself and rarely imitates, is a free man.

—Klopstock

It is better to create than to be learned; Creating is the true essence of life.

—Nieburl

If you would create something, you must be something.

—Goethe

Epilogue

This (for want of a better word) book, pamphlet, or series of thoughts is basically intended as a fun book, a thought provoker, an effort to welcome my northern friends to my homeland by kidding them (as Yankees) even as I make fun of myself (as a redneck—bigot), and an effort to communicate with future generations of my family.

Though only a very small portion of this is historical, I hope that it will encourage someone to see through the historical revisionist who sells books through creating fiction and selling it as fact. It is *your responsibility* to find the truth!

I hope that any "off color" statements or words do not offend. They have been kept to a minimum. Some things I consider funny, some folks may consider crude. That's the chance I'm willing to take as I write honestly!

June is a wonderful critic and persists in spite of the fact that I take most of her criticism personally and pout. When she's ready for us to become civil toward each other again, she just "gives me the eye, and I just melt."

I offer this book in love hoping that you will enjoy reading it as much I did writing it.

CPSIA information can be obtained at www.ICGtesting.com
Printed in the USA
LVOW120346111012

302292LV00002B/171/P

9 781479 702114